Eamonn McPolin

CCEA GCSE
MOTOR VEHICLE AND ROAD USER STUDIES
2nd Edition

COLOURPOINT EDUCATIONAL

© Eamonn McPolin and Colourpoint Books 2024

Print ISBN: 978 1 78073 384 5
eBook ISBN: 978 1 78073 385 2

Second Edition
Second Impression, 2025

Layout and design: April Sky Design
Printed by: GPS Colour Graphics Ltd

All rights reserved. No part of this publication may be reproduced, stored in a retrieval system or transmitted in any form or by any means, electronic, mechanical, photocopying, scanning, recording or otherwise, without the prior written permission of the copyright owners and publisher of this book.

Copyright has been acknowledged to the best of our ability. If there are any inadvertent errors or omissions, we shall be happy to correct them in any future editions.

Publisher's Note: This book has been written to help students preparing for the GCSE Motor Vehicle and Road User Studies specification from CCEA. While Colourpoint Educational and the author have taken every care in its production, we are not able to guarantee that the book is completely error-free. Additionally, while the book has been written to closely match the CCEA specification, it is the responsibility of each candidate to satisfy themselves that they have fully met the requirements of the CCEA specification prior to sitting an exam set by that body. For this reason, and because specifications change with time, we strongly advise every candidate to avail of a qualified teacher and to check the contents of the most recent specification for themselves prior to the exam. Colourpoint Creative Ltd therefore cannot be held responsible for any errors or omissions in this book or any consequences thereof.

Colourpoint Books
Colourpoint House
Jubilee Business Park
21 Jubilee Road
Newtownards
County Down
Northern Ireland
BT23 4YH

Tel: 028 9182 0505
E-mail: sales@colourpoint.co.uk
Web site: www.colourpointeducational.com

The Author

Eamonn McPolin graduated from St Mary's University College Belfast with a B.Ed Hons in Technology and Design. He wrote the GCSE MVRUS Scheme of Work for CCEA and is the Chief Examiner for GCSE MVRUS for an awarding body. He has twenty years' experience teaching the subject and is currently MVRUS Head of Department in St Mark's High School, Warrenpoint.

Acknowledgments

Thanks must go to a number of people for their help, support and encouragement with the production of this book. Firstly to my wife Aisling, our young family, and my mother and father for all their support, understanding and encouragement. A word of thanks to Brendan Magee (MVRUS Chair of Examiners, CCEA), Cathal McKeever (former DOE Senior Road Safety Education Officer) and Tony McDaid (MVRUS Principal Moderator, CCEA) for their for their advice and support regarding the content of this book; Donna Finlay (CCEA) for the opportunity to produce this material; and to Rachel Allen at Colourpoint for her guidance and encouragement throughout the writing process.

Picture credits

DVA: 50

Ford Company: 60 (top right), 61 (second from bottom)

Harstook: 60 (top left)

Alan Hawthorne: 13 (bottom), 18 (top), 22 (middle), 58 (top), 65 (top right and bottom left)

Highway Code: 6, 8, 9, 10 (bottom), 11 (bottom), 14 (signs), 17, 24 (top), 39 (bottom)

iStockPhoto: 3, 13 (middle), 18 (bottom), 19, 21, 22 (top and bottom), 23, 24 (bottom), 25, 26, 27, 28, 29, 33, 34, 35, 37 (bottom), 38, 39 (top), 42 (top), 46, 47 (top), 57 (top and middle), 58 (bottom left), 60 (top and bottom), 62, 63, 64 (left), 65 (bottom right), 73, 74, 75, 76, 78, 81, 82, 83, 84 (top and middle), 88, 92, 121 (top)

Malcolm Johnston: 13 (top right), 14 (top right), 37 (top), 53, 55, 66, 84 (bottom)

Norman Johnston: 57 (bottom), 58 (bottom right)

Wesley Johnston: 64 (right), 65 (top left and middle left), 67

NTEC: 68

Rachel Allen: 10 (top right), 14 (top and bottom middle)

Shutterstock: 32, 36, 42 (bottom), 47 (bottom)

All images/diagrams not listed above are ©Colourpoint Creative Ltd

CONTENTS

Chapter 1
Vehicle Control and Road User Behaviour — 6

Chapter 2
Legal Requirements — 44

Chapter 3
Road Transport and its Effect on Society — 57

Chapter 4
Motoring Mathematics — 73

Chapter 5
Collision Procedures — 82

Chapter 6
Motor Vehicle Technology — 89

Abbreviations — 128
Index — 129
Glossary — 134

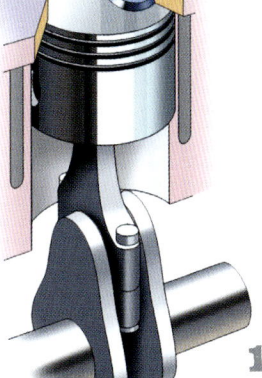

FOREWORD

Having been involved in Road Safety Education for more than 33 years I welcome wholeheartedly the publication of this book. The problem of road safety generally is one that virtually all of us have to face on a daily basis and sometimes with tragic consequences. Government Departments, Police and other Road Safety Agencies spend much time and effort dealing with the problem through education, publicity, enforcement and engineering methods. These efforts have met with a significant degree of success when one compares the fatality figures with those of earlier years. However, one has only to listen to the media to realise that tragedies still take place on our roads on a far too regular basis.

It is widely accepted that education has a major role to play in influencing attitudes and ultimately behaviour on our roads. For a number of years a GCSE in Motor Vehicle and Road User Studies (MVRUS) has been available in Northern Ireland. This has all grades status and is a serious attempt to introduce positive road user behaviour to a post primary age range, which is particularly vulnerable as drivers of either two or four wheel vehicles.

I have known Eamonn McPolin, the author of this book, since he commenced teaching the subject several years ago in St Mark's High School, Warrenpoint. He approached his teaching in a most methodical way and impressed me with his imaginative use of existing resources and indeed the production of new materials, such as student workbooks. As a consequence I asked Eamonn to speak at a Post Primary Conference in Craigavon. His contribution was described by many as 'inspirational' and there is no doubt that it helped to motivate teachers in the delivery of MVRUS in their own schools.

I am well aware of the volume of work which has gone into the production of this book. By the very nature of its diverse content, the subject of MVRUS has relied upon a wide range of resources and, very often, the teacher's own initiative. This publication has been written specifically for the recently amended Specification. It covers each of the six theory sections individually, is presented in a clear and concise manner, and has a wealth of colourful illustrations. I have no doubt that it will make a highly valuable contribution to classroom teaching and will be welcomed by all in that sector of education.

I am both delighted and honoured to write this brief foreword. During my years in road safety education I was fortunate to meet a great many highly committed and enthusiastic subject teachers. Eamonn McPolin ranks up there with the best of them and I feel sure that his work with this book will bear the fruit that it so richly deserves.

Cathal Mc Keever MBE
Former DOE Senior Road Safety Education Officer

Chapter One

VEHICLE CONTROL AND ROAD USER BEHAVIOUR

THE HIGHWAY CODE

The Highway Code is the most important book available to the road user. This book identifies the legal requirements and is well illustrated with drawings to explain the correct procedures to be followed while on the road. The main areas of the book look at:

The HIGHWAY CODE is designed to prepare learner drivers for the road

- Seat belt regulations
- Braking and stopping distances
- Correct procedures for overtaking
- Correct procedures at roundabouts
- Correct procedures when reversing
- Motorway driving
- Breakdowns and emergencies
- Road works
- Cycling requirements
- Animal regulations
- Speed limits
- Road signalling
- Signals by authorised personnel
- Traffic signs & road markings
- Vehicle markings
- Hazard warning plates

If there were no laws and rules for using the roads motorists could do whatever they wanted. This scenario would lead to more deaths, collisions, congestion and very frustrated motorists. Police and penalties both enforce the law, disciplining motorists' behaviour on the roads to improve the safety of all road users. The *Highway Code* clearly identifies the need for rules for all classes of road user – pedestrians, cyclists, motorcyclists, motorists, agricultural vehicles and horse riders. Each road user's mode of transport is different and therefore requires specific rules and behaviour.

The *Highway Code* is designed to prepare learner drivers for the road. It is also a book of rules that all motorists should refer to for advice on correct road procedures and manoeuvres. It provides the opportunity for even experienced motorists to compare their driving skills or habits to what the code actually recommends.

On passing the test, drivers are legally required to display 'R' plates for one year and drive at a restricted speed limit of 45 mph.

The driving test consists of two parts: a computerised theory element, testing the candidate's knowledge of the *Highway Code*; and a practical driving test monitored by a qualified driving examiner, who is usually based at each local Driver and Vehicle Agency (DVA) office or Ministry of Transport (MOT) test centre. Candidates must pass the theory element before taking the practical test. Before commencement of the practical driving test the candidates must be able to read a vehicle licence plate from a distance of 20 metres. The test is designed to examine learners on their knowledge of vehicle manoeuvres and on road awareness.

Upon passing the test drivers are legally required to display amber 'R' plates for one year and drive at a restricted speed limit of 45 mph. In Great Britain drivers do not have to display any plates after passing the driving test, nor is there any speed restriction. However, drivers sometimes choose to display green 'L' or 'P' plates to make other road users aware that they are new to driving unsupervised or are on a 'pass plus' scheme. In both Northern Ireland and Great Britain if drivers receive six penalty points in their first two years of driving they will automatically have to re-sit the driving test.

Advice for young drivers after passing the driving test:
- Do not drive exceeding the recommended speed limits.
- Always wear a seatbelt.
- Never show off.
- Do not use a mobile phone while driving.
- Make sure all passengers are wearing their seatbelts.
- Avoid unnecessary distractions inside your vehicle.

Road Signs

You see various traffic signs every day as you travel on the road. The signs are different colours, sizes and shapes, each with a specific meaning, direction or warning to help motorists use the roads safely. Therefore it is important to take note and obey each sign as you encounter it. The table below summarises the various types of traffic signs.

Type	Shape	Colour	Meaning
Prohibition Sign	○	Red Circle	What you must NOT do
Positive Instruction	●	Blue Circle	What you must do
Warning Sign	△	Red Triangle	Warns of possible danger
Direction Sign	M2	White Print, Blue Background	Gives directions on motorways
Direction Sign	A1	White Print, Green Background	Gives directions on primary routes
Direction Sign	Burren ↑	Black and White	Gives directions on non-primary routes
Information Sign	Loading Only	Blue and White/ Yellow and White/ Black and White	Gives information
Diversion Sign	Diversion ←	Black Print, Yellow Background	Gives information on diversion routes
Tourist Sign	Zoo →	White Print, Brown Background	Gives information for tourists

Your Highway Code book takes a closer look at all the possible road signs and it is important that you familiarise yourself with these signs.

FOR YOUR FOLDER

1. What is required to pass the driving test?
2. Name two legal requirements for motorists after passing the driving test.
3. What penalty is imposed if a restricted driver receives six penalty points in his or her first two years after passing the driving test?
4. List two pieces of advice you might give to a young driver who has just passed the driving test.
5. Study the traffic signs in your *Highway Code* book. Describe each of the traffic signs below by their type, shape, colour and meaning.

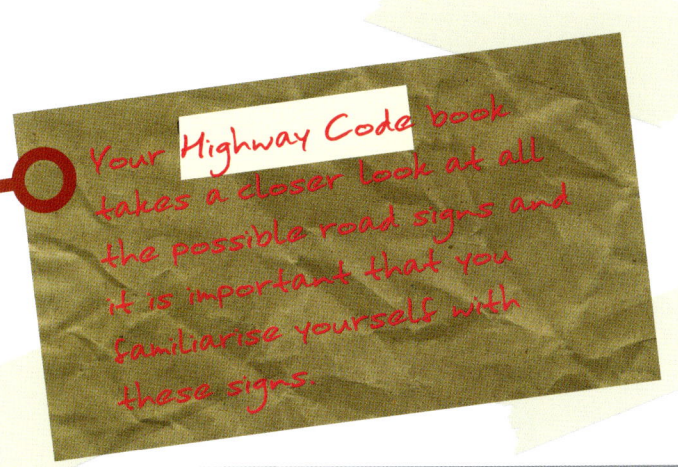

THINK

Take a look at local news stories to see if you can find any articles or notices of young drivers convicted for breaking the law. Print them out and put them in your folder under the title: 'Young drivers breaking the law on local roads'.

Signalling

Signalling, and obeying signals from signs and authorised personnel, form part of everyday driving. It is important that all drivers signal to inform others of their intentions. This reduces the risk of a collision. Similarly, it is important that all road users understand and obey any signals shown on signs, both for their own safety and for the safety of others.

Traffic lights are a common type of signal in towns and cities. Driving into a strange town or city can be a daunting task if you are not sure where you are going, so leave early, take your time and drive carefully. On dual-carriageways and motorways you must be aware of electronic signs and signals for speed limits, directions, weather conditions, diversions and road works.

Study the signals listed below in your Highway Code book:
- Traffic light signals
- Motorway signals
- Signals by authorised personnel
- Arm signals to other road users

Signals given by authorised persons

When driving on the roads there are three groups of people whose signals we must obey. They are the:

- Police (PSNI)
- Driver and Vehicle Agency Enforcement Officer (DVA Enforcement Officer)
- Customs and Excise Officers

When might the Police signal?

- At a road check point
- To ease traffic flow
- At a collision scene
- To divert traffic
- At large events

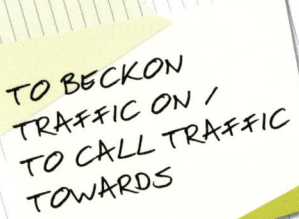

TO BECKON TRAFFIC ON / TO CALL TRAFFIC TOWARDS

10

DVA Enforcement Officers are responsible for enforcing a wide range of legislation about goods vehicles, taxis, private cars, buses and agricultural vehicles. DVA Enforcement Officers are employed to carry out checks on vehicles using the roads to ensure they comply with legislation. One such example is ensuring vehicles using the road have paid vehicle excise duty (VED). For more information check Roadside Compliance on the NI Direct website. Customs and Excise Officers also use signals to stop or direct vehicles to the hard shoulder at fuel fraud checkpoints, usually found on main roads. These officers have the authority to fine drivers and impound their vehicles if they are found to be using illegal fuel.

Primary and secondary signals

Primary light signals refer to the traffic lights that you are waiting at. If you can see further traffic light signals ahead these are secondary light signals.

The pictures (right) show the correct order for the way traffic lights work:
A. Stop
B. Stop – Do not pass until green shows
C. Go
D. Stop

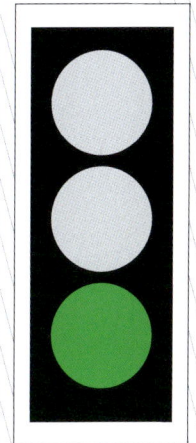

Signals given by drivers and others

When driving, you must remember to signal by using your indicators to tell other motorists, pedestrians, motorcyclists, cyclists, agricultural vehicles and horse riders what you intend to do or where you intend to go. You have to remember that other road users are watching for your signals at road junctions and roundabouts. Failure to signal can cause other road users to become frustrated or misjudge your intentions. In the event that your lights and indicators fail while driving it is important that you use the arm signals shown on the right instead. Unauthorised persons may only use signals to stop and divert traffic to warn of a collision or hazard ahead until an authorised body such as the police arrive at the scene to take over.

I intend to move out to the right or turn right

I intend to move in to the left or turn left

I intend to slow down or stop

I intend to move in to the left or turn left

I intend to move out to the right or turn right

I intend to slow down or stop

FOR YOUR FOLDER

1. Why is it important to signal properly on the road?
2. What three groups of authorised personnel must we obey when they signal?
3. Draw the traffic light signals in the correct order starting with Go.
4. What does a red and amber traffic light mean?
5. What does amber on its own mean?

THINK

Using the Internet research the work of the traffic police and answer the following:
- Briefly describe the work of the traffic police.
- There are two types of fixed penalty fines. What are they? Explain their differences.

Each set of road markings has a specific meaning. Some motorists ignore road markings because they simply do not understand what they mean. This could lead to serious consequences, either in the form of a collision or penalty points being awarded to the motorist because of dangerous driving.

All road markings have different meanings. Two main colours are used on roads – white and yellow. White is used most and found on all roads. Yellow is mainly used to indicate restrictions, such as those regarding parking and loading.

Your *Highway Code* book looks at road markings in more detail. It is important that you investigate these further.

Give way to traffic on a major road

Give way to traffic from right at roundabout

Give way to traffic from right at mini-roundabout

Stop line on most roads

No waiting at any time

12

Safe grip is another coloured material used on roads. It is usually a rough material, creamy yellow, red or green in colour.

Creamy yellow
Usually found at a bad bend or corner or on approach to a roundabout. Helps motorists to grip and slow down.

Green
Usually found on cycle tracks.

Red
Usually found in built up or residential areas to indicate a speed limit of 30 mph.

Rumble Strips

Rumble strips (shown on the right) are road markings designed to alert inattentive drivers by causing audible vibration to pass through the wheels to the inside of the vehicle. Rumble strips are often found as an edge line along the side of a road to alert drivers when they are crossing it, particularly when falling asleep or not paying attention to road position.

Road Studs

To assist drivers on motorways at night, road studs were introduced to help them identify their road position more easily. Each colour of stud marks a specific position.
- **Amber** – marks the right-hand edge of the carriageway or central reservation.
- **Red** – marks the left-hand edge of the carriageway.
- **Green** – separates slip roads from the motorway and indicates side roads or turn-offs on carriageways.
- **Cat's Eye** – (shown on the right) marks the centre line on a single-carriageway and the middle lanes on motorways.

It is also important not to forget about the other types of road and vehicle markings that you may come across, such as:

- Waiting restrictions
- Loading restrictions
- Zebra crossings
- School patrols
- Bus lanes
- Hazard warning plates

You should look at these more closely in your Highway Code book.

FOR YOUR FOLDER

1. On a motorway, reflective studs are inserted to indicate different road positions at night. In your folder copy out the key below and fill in the blanks to match the road stud colours (red, green, orange, white) with the correct road position.

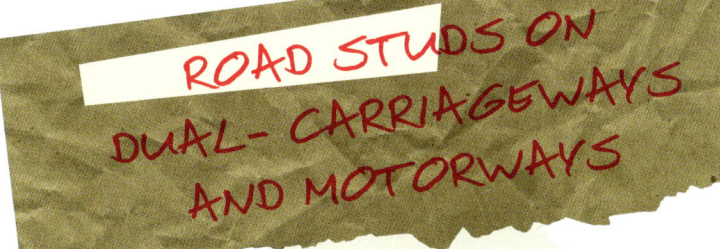

ROAD STUDS ON DUAL-CARRIAGEWAYS AND MOTORWAYS

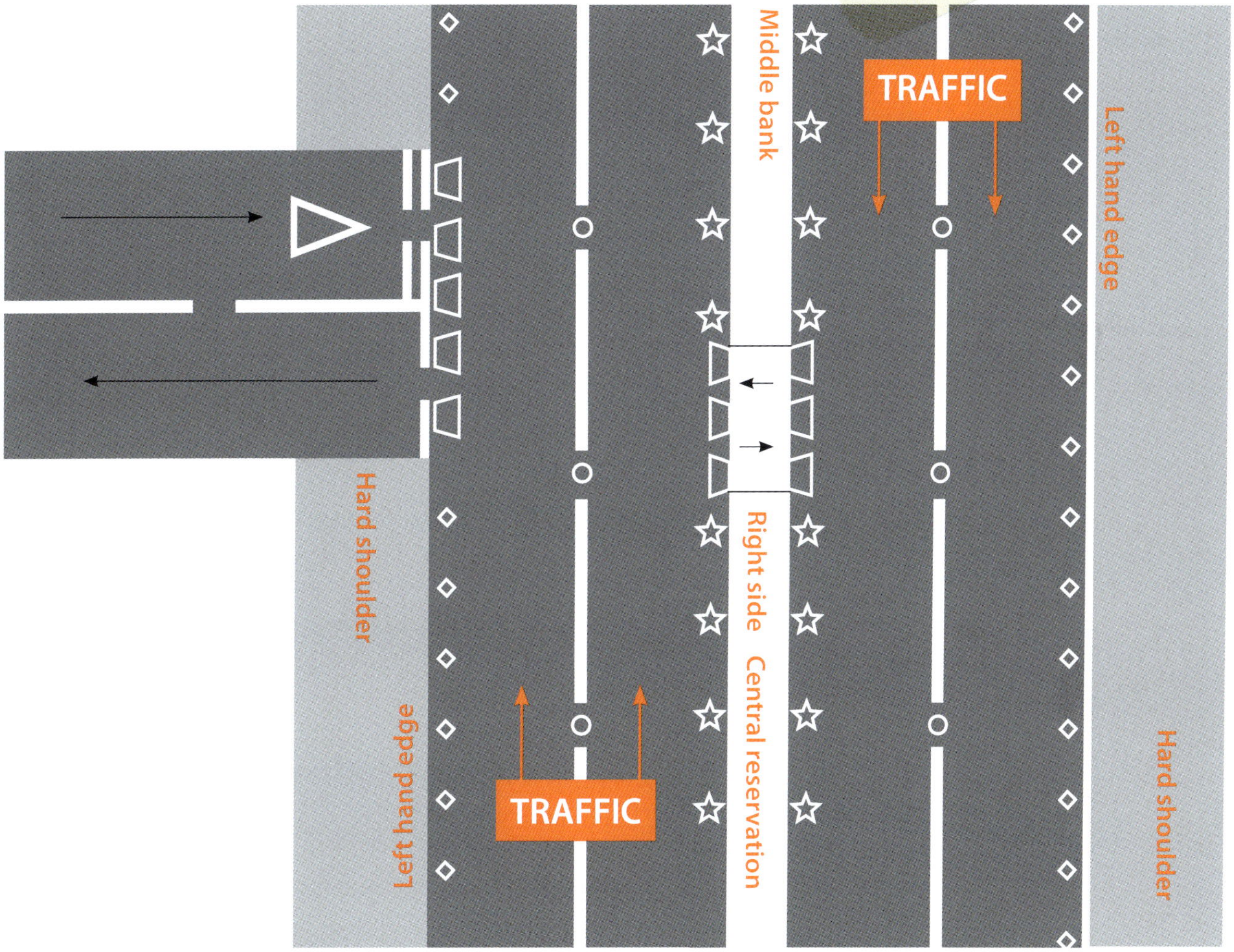

○ _____ eyes separate the traffic lanes

◇ _____ studs mark the hard shoulder or left hand edge

◁ _____ studs mark a side or slip road

☆ _____ studs mark the right hand edge or central reservation

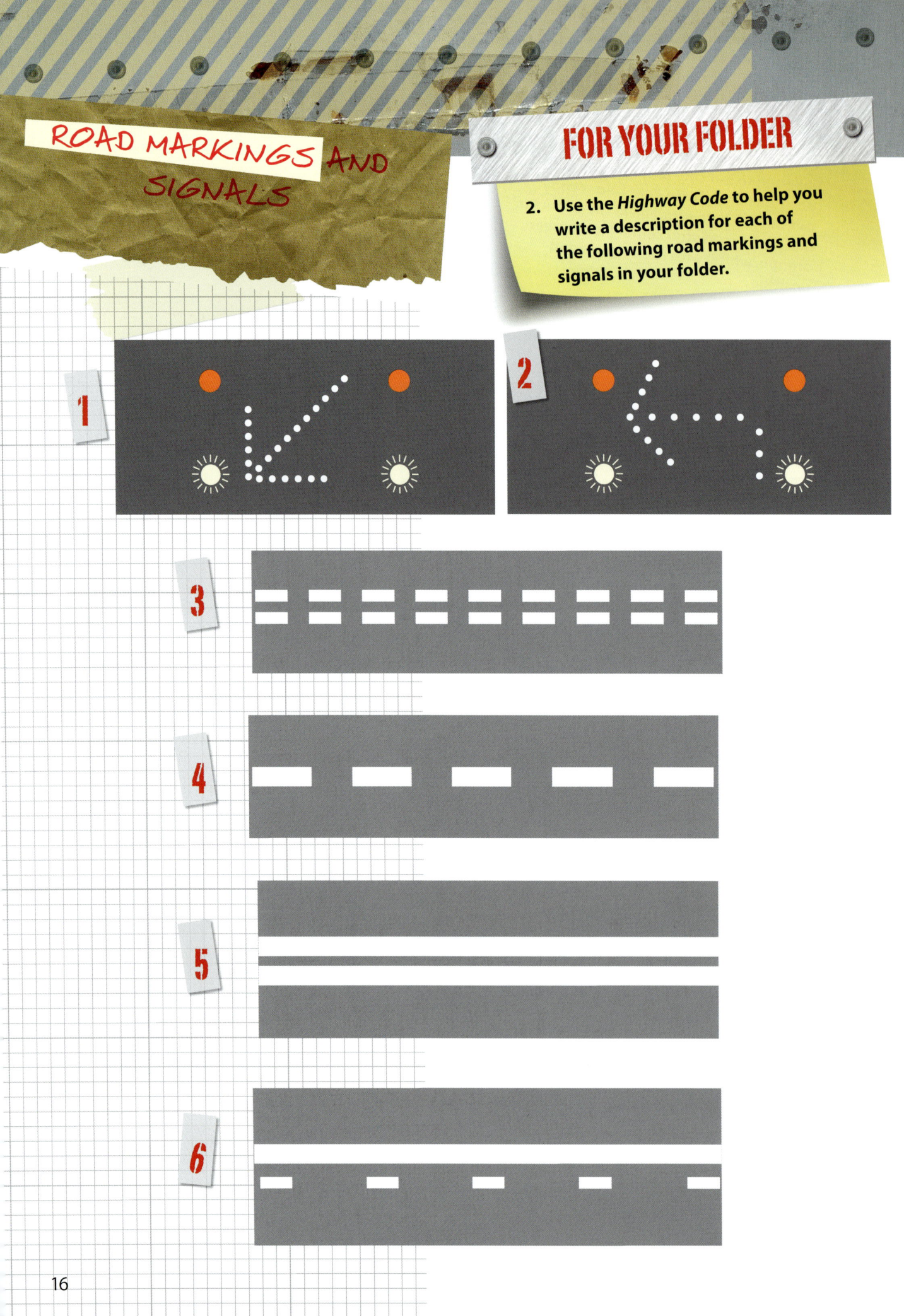

Vehicle Manoeuvring

Highlighted below are some of the main manoeuvres you will have to make if driving a vehicle. It is important that you study each of these sections properly in your *Highway Code* book to fully inform yourself of the correct procedures.

ROAD JUNCTIONS

There are a number of different types of road junction.

At a road junction, you need to slow down or stop before entering another road. You need to take extra care at junctions, checking your position and speed when approaching them. Always make sure you check your mirrors and indicate in plenty of time before pulling out (mirror, signal, manoeuvre). Junctions are particularly dangerous for cyclists, motorcyclists and pedestrians, so watch out for them before you pull out or turn in.

Box junctions are a traffic control system set up to prevent traffic congestion at busy road junctions. These are usually identified as large, yellow boxes with criss-cross lines. Vehicles are not allowed to stop inside the box. These junctions are designed to allow motorists to move whenever their exit route is clear and to allow motorists to turn right safely.

Junctions controlled by traffic lights stop vehicles to allow pedestrians to cross roads safely. They also ease traffic congestion as each exit route is given a set amount of time to allow traffic through.

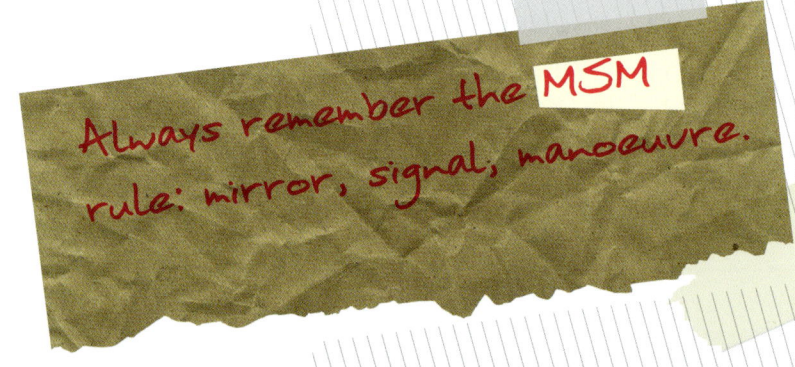

Always remember the MSM rule: mirror, signal, manoeuvre.

Roundabouts

When approaching a roundabout it is important to decide as early as possible which exit you need to take and get into the correct lane using the mirror, signal, manoeuvre rule. You must always give way to traffic on your right and should be especially aware of motorists who are already on the roundabout.

The blind spot

Blind spots are the parts of the road that you cannot see from the driving seat, even with use of your mirrors. Head restraints in the back of a vehicle can impair a driver's vision when reversing and the door panels between the front and rear side windows can also obstruct a driver's vision when overtaking.

Reversing

Before reversing make sure there are no pedestrians, particularly children, or obstructions on the road behind you. Check your blind spot behind you. You should only reverse your vehicle for as long as is absolutely necessary.

Overtaking

You must keep in the left-hand lane unless you are overtaking. You overtake only on the right, unless traffic is moving in queues and the queue on your right is moving more slowly than you are. You must not use the hard shoulder to overtake.

To overtake you should drop back from the vehicle in front so that you can get a clear look at the road ahead. Driving too close to the vehicle in front is referred to as tailgating. Take time to judge the speeds of any traffic on the road and take special care at night when visibility is poorer and distances are more difficult to judge. Check your mirrors, indicate in plenty of time, and then pull out (mirror, signal, manoeuvre). You need to double check before pulling out to overtake that no vehicles or motorcyclists are approaching quickly behind you. When you have pulled out accelerate past the slower moving vehicle. To pull back in you must again check your mirrors and indicate. Be sure not to pull back in too quickly as you may force the vehicle that you have passed to brake suddenly.

Road works

Special care is needed at road works. Watch out for and follow all the signs on the approach to and at the road works. They are often a cause of frustration for motorists and can lead to impatient manoeuvres. Where you know there are going to be road works you should allow more time for your journey to compensate for any delays.

Breakdowns

If you break down on the motorway, pull onto the hard shoulder. On any other road, if possible, remove your car from the road and put on your hazard lights to warn others of your presence.

FOR YOUR FOLDER

Look at the 'Overtaking' section in your *Highway Code* book. Answer the following questions in relation to this section.

1. On what side of the road do you overtake on?
2. If you see solid double white lines down the centre of a road, what do these mean?
3. Before overtaking what three checks should you make?
4. What three precautions must you take when overtaking large vehicles?
5. Name three instances where it may be unsafe to pass if you cannot see far enough ahead.
6. Why is it important not to cut in too quickly in front of another vehicle when overtaking?

FOR YOUR FOLDER

Look at the 'Roundabouts' section in your *Highway Code* book. Answer the following questions in relation to this section.

1. On reaching a roundabout, priority must be given to whom?
2. State two actions that a motorist needs to take on approach to a roundabout.
3. State two things that you must do before exiting a roundabout.
4. Why is it important to indicate at a roundabout?
5. Why is it important to be aware of motorists that are already on the roundabout?

CAUSES AND PREVENTION OF ROAD COLLISIONS

There is a very good chance that you could be present at the scene of a road traffic collision at some stage in your life. Statistics drawn up over the years have highlighted that drivers and passengers in vehicles have a 10% chance of being involved in a collision sometime within their life span. Every year the police, NISRA and Stormont Executive produce sets of statistics relating to road traffic collisions in Northern Ireland. Statistics produced include the number of deaths on the roads, seat belt wearing rates and drink driving prosecutions. These figures are used to indicate problem areas that need to be addressed. The police may tackle target areas or publicity campaigns may follow to increase awareness of a deteriorating situation.

We all use the roads as a means to get to wherever we need to go. No matter how you are travelling, whether in a vehicle or on foot, it should be done safely so that you do not risk our own lives or those of others. It is very important that you always concentrate fully on the road ahead, as a moment's lapse in concentration could be life threatening. Survivors of collisions who know they are responsible come up with all types of explanations and excuses. However, nine out of ten collisions are caused by some mistake or misjudgement by the driver or individual.

The two most likely categories of drivers to have collisions are the young and elderly – those under the age of twenty-five and those who are over sixty-five. Among young drivers the main causes of road collisions are speeding or drinking and driving. Elderly people sometimes make misjudgements as a result of their failing eyesight and hearing. A few of the main collision causes are listed opposite.

collision causes

- High risk areas
- Adverse weather conditions
- Physical and mental fitness of the driver
- Vulnerable road users
- Distractions
- Speeding

All collisions are costly, not only because of damage expenses but also the even greater cost of death or serious injury. Unfortunately some families are forced to deal with unexpected and unnecessary deaths. Some people do survive road collisions but are left severely injured with limited quality of life, having to depend on others for support and survival. You probably know how difficult it is to watch some of the road safety advertisements on TV and hope that similar scenarios never happen to you.

High Risk Areas

On public roads there are a number of areas that have a high risk of road traffic collisions. You need to be very careful and aware of the possible dangers that can arise when approaching the following:

- **A bad bend** – You should slow down when approaching a bad bend because if you lose control of your vehicle you could end up on the other side of the road, which could cause a collision with oncoming traffic. Travelling at speed around a corner could also lead to your vehicle toppling or rolling over onto its side or roof.

- **A brow of a hill** – You should reduce your speed when approaching the brow of a hill because your forward vision will be restricted. You should anticipate possible hazards on the other side of the brow and be prepared to slow down or stop if required.

- **A hidden dip** – Dips in the road are often hidden. It is common to think you can see the entire road ahead and pull out to pass a slow moving vehicle. This is very dangerous because if you meet an oncoming vehicle you will be unprepared and could cause a head-on collision. You should only pull out to pass if the road ahead is straight and clear of traffic.

- **A residential area** – In residential areas there are often children playing in the street and sometimes dogs or cats running loose. Children and animals are not very aware of the dangers of the road and could run out in front of your vehicle. This could force you to brake or swerve suddenly, which could cause any traffic behind you to collide with the back of your vehicle. If you are very unlucky you might even hit the child or animal. Therefore it is important to drive slowly and carefully when travelling through residential areas. Parked cars are also a problem as a pedestrian crossing between them would not have a clear view of the road and could step out in front of your passing vehicle. Similarly, someone opening a car door without checking the traffic could cause a collision, as you would have to brake or swerve suddenly to avoid the door. If you are parked along the side of a road you should always check your mirrors for approaching traffic before getting out of your vehicle.

a residential area...

Certain times of the day have an increased risk of collisions because of greater vehicle and pedestrian activity, such as the following:

7-9 am people going to work and school
3-4 pm schools closing
5-6 pm people going home from work
school/religious/bank holidays

Schools in particular can add to congestion, with buses and parents leaving and collecting their children. School opening and closing times will also increase pedestrian movement. If driving at these times you need to be vigilant, as school children may dash across a road to catch up with friends or to catch their bus. The start and end of a working day will also increase traffic congestion. Between the working hours of 8 am and 6 pm there may be an increased number of vans and lorries on the roads doing deliveries. Holiday periods will also increase traffic on the roads, especially in good weather, because people will want to take trips with their families or go shopping, to make the most of their free time. This may lead to congestion in specific places such as good shopping towns, country parks or seaside resorts.

Adverse Weather Conditions

Weather hazards cause many problems for drivers. You must be aware of the different ways in which each type of weather can affect the road conditions and your driving manoeuvres. You should then be able to drive safely and cope with any problems that are presented to you. Pedestrians are also affected by changes in weather conditions. Weather hazards such as fog, snow, ice, wind and rain are the main problems as they affect hearing, vision and balance. Driving at night also has its problems.

Equipment

It is important that both pedestrians and cyclists make themselves as visible as possible on the roads, especially in poor conditions. Bright, fluorescent or reflective clothing should be worn on some part of the body so that they stand out when the lights of a passing vehicle shine on them.

Fluorescent materials work better in daylight because they react to sunlight's ultraviolet rays, causing fluorescent glare and making it stand out against its background. Fluorescent materials come in orange, yellow or lime green colours. At night or when visibility is poor, fluorescent materials are less noticeable and therefore reflective materials are used instead. Reflective materials work best at night and reflect the light produced by vehicle headlights straight back at the driver. Thousands of tiny, shiny beads in the material act in a similar way to the white cats eyes on the road, its reflective properties directing the light straight back at the driver. Clothing is available that combines both fluorescent and reflective properties. Pedestrians, cyclists, motorcyclists and horse riders should use a range of reflective aids to make them more noticeable on the roads, such as reflectors on bicycles, reflective stickers, reflective and fluorescent armbands, hats, helmets and other items of clothing.

Cold weather equipment

During the winter months additional emergency equipment should be carried in a car. Some of this equipment is listed opposite.

Rain

The main problem for road users in the rain is poor visibility. Heavy rain and spray from other vehicles can be constant and difficult to clear quickly with windscreen wipers. Wet roads require increased braking distances and tyres have less grip because water makes the road surface greasy and slippery. To drive safely you should drive slowly, with dipped headlights, making sure that your windows are clear and not misted over. By driving slowly the vehicle will have more grip on the road as the tyre treads will be able to remove a greater amount of surface water. Driving too fast will not allow the treads the opportunity to disperse enough water, leading to reduced grip. As tyre treads are needed to disperse the water and keep a grip on the road surface, badly-worn tyres can also cause road traffic collisions in wet conditions due to the reduced tread depth. When driving in wet conditions you must also remember that braking and stopping distances will be at least doubled as a result of the reduced tyre grip. The brakes will not be as effective as they would be in dry conditions because they will be wet and need drying out. Brake pads that are wet are more likely to allow the discs and drums to continue slipping instead of bringing them to a halt. To compensate for these conditions you need to drive much slower, apply the brakes gently and allow time for your vehicle to stop.

Pedestrians may be more difficult to see in wet conditions and should ideally wear fluorescent or reflective clothing. Wet clothing is generally dull and harder for motorists to see, as well as being heavy and affecting pedestrians' speed. Rain drowns out noise, making it more difficult to hear oncoming traffic and pedestrians may tend to cross roads in a hurry to get out of the rain. Remember hoods and umbrellas keep you dry but reduce hearing and visibility. When driving you must thus be very aware of pedestrians walking alongside or crossing roads, as their hearing and visibility may be impaired, and they may be more inclined to lose their balance as surfaces can be very slippery under foot.

First aid kit (bandages)
De-icer spray
Jump leads
Torch
Reflective jacket
Mobile phone
Blanket and chocolate in case you are stranded

Aquaplaning

Tyre treads are used to remove rain and surface water to increase tyre grip with the road surface. Driving at a high speed makes it more difficult to remove a large volume of rain and surface water. Therefore a vehicle's grip on the road may be greatly reduced, causing the wheels to lift up off the road onto the top of the surface water. This in turn causes brakes and steering to be less effective and will be improved only if the vehicle's speed is reduced. Aquaplaning occurs as a result of excessive speed and standing surface water.

Flooded roads

If you have to drive through very deep water you should drive carefully but not too slowly as this may result in your engine stalling and it could prove difficult to re-start. However, if you drive too quickly you may get water in the engine or the electrics, which could lead to very serious and expensive damage. After driving through deep water you should test your brakes. If they have water on them they may need drying out. You are most likely to drive into a flood at night when visibility is poor. You should never drive through water that is more than 250 mm deep. The safest option is always to try and find an alternative route.

Sun

We all enjoy the good weather and sunny conditions. However, the sun's brightness can blind road users and impair their driving. Similarly, sun shining after a shower of rain can reflect off the wet road causing poor visibility. Silver vehicles in particular are harder to see when the sun is shining. Sun that is blocked from reaching the road surface can form deep shadows, causing dullness, and a pedestrian walking along the side of the road in this deep shadow may be difficult for motorists to see.

You should wear sunglasses and use your sun visor to improve your vision and block out the sun's glare when driving. In winter the sun is lower in the sky and sun visors do not provide as much protection as they would in the summer months. If you have to drive a long distance in warm weather it is important to keep your vehicle well ventilated by either winding the window down or turning on the air conditioning. This will help prevent you from becoming drowsy.

Driving at night

Dawn and dusk are the two most difficult times to drive, when it is neither bright nor dark. It is easier to see vehicles in the light of day and on a clear dark night when lights are clearly visible. Before setting out on a journey, you should make sure that all your lights, both front and rear, are in full working order. This is one of the checks carried out during the MOT. It is used to check that a vehicle's lights are focused and aligned properly, to ensure the clearest and brightest vision of the road ahead. One problem with driving at night is the blinding lights of approaching and passing vehicles. If driving a

DRIVING AT NIGHT...

long distance, these conditions can be extremely tiring on the eyes, especially for older motorists. Therefore it is important that you are considerate and dip you headlights when approaching or following other vehicles because the brightness of a full beam can be blinding. The full beam should be used *only* when the road ahead is clear. Motorists often use their headlights to 'flash' at other vehicles to indicate some form of a warning: for example, if the road ahead has animals running loose on it.

Another common hazard for motorists in the dark is that poor light makes it more difficult to judge the speed and distance of other vehicles. It is therefore very important to take extra care, especially when pulling out of a side road or junction. You should be particularly aware of lighting up times. The 'Lighting requirements' section in the *Highway Code* clearly states that vehicle lights must be switched on half an hour after sunset and half an hour before sunrise. What you have to remember is that where there are no street lights, vision will be restricted to the range of your vehicle's headlights. Therefore vehicle speed must be reduced to compensate for the lack of forward vision. Parking at night is another major problem for motorists and is addressed in detail in the 'Parking at night' section in your *Highway Code* book. You should take a few minutes to read these laws in greater detail.

Fog

Fog causes poor visibility for all types of road user. When driving in fog you should always drive slowly, using dipped headlights, along with front and rear fog lights. Fog lights are very strong and can blind other motorists if used in dry or clear conditions. Therefore they must only be used when visibility is poor. Fog comes and goes, it can be thick in one place and thin in another, and can therefore catch road users off guard. On a straight part of the road visibility could be very good and suddenly, around the next corner, visibility could be very poor as a result of scattered fog. Fog can affect a road user's sight and hearing. This not only makes it harder to see other vehicles but also to judge their speed and distance. When pulling out of a side road or junction in fog, you should wind down the window because listening for vehicles can sometimes be easier than seeing them. Sometimes you may even need to sound your horn to make others aware of your presence. As in wet conditions, pedestrians may be more difficult to see and their hearing may be impaired in the fog. Fluorescent or reflective clothing will make them more visible to motorists but it is essential that they take more time to look and listen for traffic when crossing the road.

Fog is a major cause of motorway collisions because of the fast-moving nature of the road. You must slow down and take extra time on these roads during foggy weather to reduce the risk of having a collision. Vehicles without rear fog lights and vehicles parked along the side of a road can be difficult to see in fog when approached from behind.

How to drive safely in fog:
fog code...

- Slow down
- Keep a safe distance from the vehicle in front
- Never follow the lights or trust the manoeuvres of the vehicle in front of you
- Always use dipped headlights
- Use your wipers and keep your window clear
- Roll down your window to listen for traffic
- Leave plenty of time for your journey

Snow

Snow can make travelling very difficult. A large amount of fresh falling snow that lies can grind the movement of all road vehicles to a halt. Road conditions usually become wet and slippery causing vehicle handling to be more difficult, especially steering and braking, which can cause vehicles to spin out of control. In such conditions you should take extra care, drive and manoeuvre slowly, use dipped headlights, avoid sudden braking, and stay well back from the vehicle in front to allow for greater braking and stopping distances. Climbing hills in snow can also be difficult and should be done in a low gear, as tyres find it difficult to grip the road. Snow can build up quickly on vehicle windscreens, reducing visibility, and in the wheel arches, making it difficult for the tyres to rotate. It is important that both are cleared before setting out on a journey.

How to drive safely in
snow...

- Drive slowly in a low gear and manoeuvre smoothly
- Keep a safe distance from the vehicle in front
- Gently test your brakes
- Use dipped headlights in falling snow
- Keep your windscreen and lights clear

Ice

Frost and ice can cause major problems for motorists, as roads can become very slippery, causing vehicle handling to be more difficult. Frost can be identified by a sparkling white colour on the ground. You should always check the road for ice if you suspect slippery conditions before setting out in your vehicle. If it is frosty or icy you should reduce your speed, avoid heavy breaking and allow more time for your journey. Braking and stopping distances should be at least doubled in these conditions, to assist the vehicle in coming safely to a stop in a controlled manner. All vehicles should carry a de-icer spray, especially during the winter months, to clear windscreens of frost. These conditions also pose major problems for motorcyclists as they travel on two wheels not four. Any slippage in these conditions could cause a motorcycle to spiral out of control.

Black ice is dangerous because it is tricky to spot and often catches motorists off-guard. It is caused by rain falling and freezing on an already frost covered surface. This makes it difficult to see and it is often mistaken for a wet patch or puddle. Motorists are often on top of it before they realise and end up braking heavily causing the vehicle to slide even more. It is even more difficult to see in the dark.

Strong winds

You should never underestimate the power of the wind. No matter what type of road you are on, as a motorist, pedestrian or cyclist, you can still be affected by the wind. On country roads trees and branches often fall causing obstructions or more serious damage if they land on top of a vehicle. When gale force winds are blowing you are advised to stay indoors and not drive unless it is absolutely necessary. In towns and cities strong winds can blow litter about, distracting motorists' attention. Pedestrians waiting to cross a road may be blown out into the path of moving traffic by a strong gust. On open, exposed roads, such as motorways and bridges, crosswinds can be a major problem, causing vehicles to sway, especially when turning corners or overtaking.

It is very important that when driving in stormy conditions you drive slowly so that you have full control of your vehicle and its steering. Articulated lorries, cars towing trailers, vehicles with roof racks and high-sided vehicles are particularly at risk in strong winds. This is because their increased length or height is more likely to catch the wind, which could cause further steering problems or even tip the vehicles over. You need to be particularly aware of wind that is funnelled through gaps. This is when wind is forced to travel through a confined area, concentrating the wind's power and increasing its strength. Drivers, cyclists and pedestrians can often be caught unawares by funnelled winds. For example, a sheltered road could have one open place that the wind blows through, causing vehicles to sway or cyclists to topple over. Side streets and alleyways can also cause funnelled winds, particularly affecting pedestrians. Headwinds mostly affect cyclists, pedestrians and motorcyclists, where the wind blows against them, restricting and slowing their movement.

Adverse weather conditions summarised

Condition	Effects on driver	What should you do?
Rain	• Reduces visibility and increases braking distances. • Tyres have less grip. • Pedestrians wear hoods and umbrellas in the rain. This decreases their vision and hearing, which may result in them walking out in front of a car. • Roads become very slippy.	• Reduce speed: the slower you drive the more grip you have. • Use dipped headlights. • Clear condensation off the windows using the demister and headed screen element. • Wear reflective clothing.
Aquaplaning	• This is when the tyres rise up off the road onto the top of surface water caused by heavy rain. • Causes the steering and brakes to become ineffective, making the driver lose control of the vehicle.	• Reduce speed immediately.
Flooded roads	• More likely to drive into a flood at night when visibility is poor. • If driving too fast your car might come to a violent stop allowing water to damage the engine. If driving too slowly your vehicle may stall and be difficult to restart. • Brakes become wet and ineffective.	• Do not drive through water that is more than 250 mm deep. • Drive slowly through shallow floods so that the electrics in the engine do not get damaged.
Sun	• Blinds road users. • Reduces visibility. • Sun reflects off wet roads. • Warm weather can make a driver drowsy. • Sun that is blocked from the road can create dullness and deep shadows.	• Wear tinted sunglasses and use sun visors. • Keep vehicles well ventilated.
Driving at night	• Lights of other road users can be blinding. • Difficult to judge the speed and distance of other vehicles. • Where there is no street lighting your vision is restricted to the range of your headlights.	• Drive at a slower speed. • Dipped headlights should be used at dusk. • Dipped headlights should be used when approaching other vehicles. • Check all lights before setting off on a journey.
Fog	• Reduces visibility not only for you but for everyone. • It also muffles noise. • Vehicles with no rear fog lights and vehicles parked along the side of roads can be difficult to see. • It is hard to judge the speed and distance of other vehicles.	• Always use dipped headlights and fog lights both front and back. • Drive slowly. • When turning out of a road open the window and listen out for approaching vehicles. • Sometimes you may need to sound the horn. • Follow the fog code.

Ice	• Roads can become slippy and the car becomes harder to control. • Braking and stopping distances can be increased. • Black ice (surface water which freezes on the top of the road) is difficult to see and is often mistaken for a wet patch, catching many drivers unaware.	• Check the road for ice before starting out on a journey. • Look out for sparkling reflections which indicate frost. • Reduce speed and allow more time for your journey. • Drive slowly and avoid heavy braking.
Snow	• Causes roads to become slippery. • Reduces visibility as it builds up on the window screen and headlights. • Wheel arches can be blocked restricting wheel movement. • Can grind all movement to a halt. • Vehicle handling and steering can become more difficult because roads are slippy. • Braking and stopping distances can be increased.	• Use dipped headlights in falling snow. • Drive and manoeuvre slowly, staying well back from the vehicle in front. • Going up and down hills should be done in a low gear. • Clear windscreens, lights and wheel arches before setting off.
Strong winds	• Rubbish blowing in towns distracts drivers' attention. • On rural roads, falling branches and trees can be a problem. • On exposed roads, such as motorways and bridges, crosswinds can affect the handling of a vehicle. • Headwinds restrict and slow the movement of cyclists and pedestrians.	• Reduce speeds so that you can comfortably cope with the steering of the vehicle. • Be wary of passing high-sided vehicles as they could sway into your path.

FOR YOUR FOLDER

1. Why is fog considered to be a major cause of motorway collisions?
2. How does fog affect a driver?
3. Make a list of procedures you should follow in foggy conditions.
4. Why is it important to keep a vehicle well ventilated in the warm weather?
5. How does the sun affect a driver's sight?
6. Why is the sun a greater hazard in winter?
7. State two reasons why it is important for motorists to reduce their speed in wet weather.
8. How can motorists make themselves more visible on the roads?
9. Why are pedestrians vulnerable in wet conditions?
10. List four things a motorist can do to improve his or her own safety when driving in snow.

FOR YOUR FOLDER

1. What is black ice?
2. State two things a driver could do to reduce the risk of a collision in icy conditions.
3. What does the term aquaplaning mean?
4. How is a motorist affected by aquaplaning?
5. Name two precautions a driver should take when approaching a flood.
6. Where are strong winds most dangerous to motorists?
7. Why are high-sided vehicles vulnerable in strong winds?
8. How do strong winds affect a motorist in a town or city?
9. Why is it important to dip your headlights when approaching other vehicles?
10. Make a list of equipment needed in cold weather.

THE PHYSICAL AND MENTAL FITNESS OF THE DRIVER

Alcohol

People drink for various different reasons. It may be to celebrate a special occasion, to be sociable, or even to release stress or worry. Many of the effects of drinking alcohol that make people feel relaxed and happy can also impair their driving skills. Your chances of having a road collision are much higher when under the influence of alcohol because drinking alcohol affects your body in the following ways:

- You cannot coordinate and control your muscles as well as you can normally because alcohol is a depressant.
- It takes you longer to react, so it is more difficult to deal with the unexpected.
- It impairs your decision-making process.
- You are less able to judge speed and distance.
- You are often more daring and reckless, making you more likely to drive fast.

Alcohol is broken down and dispersed by the liver, and eating before and after drinking further slows down this process. There is no fast way to remove alcohol from the bloodstream.

What people sometimes forget is that all drinks have different strengths, that will affect them in different ways and at different speeds. Many people think that it is safe and legal to have one drink and drive. It is not that simple. Different measures of drink contain different amounts of alcohol. The current level for

KEY POINTS – LEGAL LIMITS

35 micrograms of alcohol per 100 millilitres of breath
80 milligrams of alcohol per 100 millilitres of blood
107 milligrams of alcohol per 100 millilitres of urine

There are two laws regarding drink driving:

BEING OVER THE LIMIT

DRIVING UNDER THE INFLUENCE

Driving after any intake of alcohol leaves you open to prosecution. This is usually a hefty fine and disqualification. The simplest rule to follow is:

**IF YOU DRIVE, DON'T DRINK,
IF YOU DRINK, DON'T DRIVE.**

a drink drive prosecution is 35 micrograms of alcohol per 100 millilitres of breath. Another method used to determine alcohol levels is Blood Alcohol Concentration (BAC). This method determines the amount of alcohol in the bloodstream after consuming beverages.

If any of the above legal limits are exceeded it is likely that the courts will disqualify a driver for a minimum of 12 months. Having a drink-driving disqualification may ultimately lead to further implications for the offender, such as higher insurance premiums. If employed as a lorry or taxi driver it may even lead to the loss of a job.

On average, it takes about one hour to remove one unit of alcohol from the body. However the rate does vary from person to person and can depend on your weight, whether you are male or female, how much you have eaten and the general condition of your liver.

Drugs

Unfortunately in our society today there is an increasing demand for drugs. When drugs are mentioned, generally people think of illegal drugs, such as cocaine, ecstasy, heroine and marijuana. What they do not realise is that drugs prescribed by hospitals, doctors and chemists, such as painkillers, tranquillisers and sleeping pills, can also have side effects that can affect their judgement and reactions. Therefore if taking any sort of a medication you must make sure you read the instructions on the box or bottle before taking a vehicle out onto the roads. You must remember that you will be putting yourself and other motorists at risk if you decide to drive under the influence of drugs. Therefore the police and courts will not be sympathetic if you are caught under this influence and will usually impose a large fine, penalty points or driving licence disqualification.

Fatigue (tiredness)

When you are tired your reactions are slower and less effective. A number of factors can cause you to become tired. A few of these are listed below:

- Distance (in the length of journey)
- Warm weather
- Boredom of traffic delays
- Monotony of motorway driving

It is very important that you keep the vehicle well ventilated and stop often to refresh yourself when travelling long distances, as this should help reduce the effects of tiredness. If travelling by car with another adult who is insured on the vehicle it is a good idea to share the driving. Using a route planner prior to setting off allows you to plan your journey, which should help you arrive at your destination as quickly, and hopefully as stress-free, as possible.

FOR YOUR FOLDER

1. State three ways that alcohol affects the body.
2. Why do different drinks affect the body in different ways?
3. Is alcohol a stimulant or a depressant?
4. How is alcohol dispersed from the blood stream?
5. Why should people not drink and drive?
6. What are the three legal limits for drinking and driving?
7. What could happen to a driver found over the legal limit?

THINK

1. Take a look at this week's local news for incidents where people have been prosecuted for drink driving.
2. Look at the penalty points table in your *Highway Code* book.
List the two drinking and driving offences and the main differences between their penalties.

Vision

As you get older your eyesight may let you down. Unless you take the time to visit the opticians, it will only be tested once in your driving life – when taking your first driving test. During your first driving test the vehicle test examiner will ask and expect you to be able to read a vehicle registration plate from a distance of 20.5 metres.

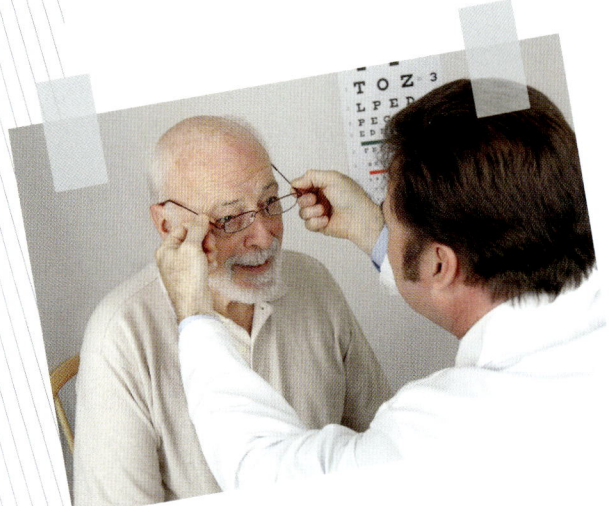

Your vision can be affected in two main ways:

1. **Peripheral vision** relates to your side vision. This refers to your ability to see objects and movements that could become a hazard outside of your direct line of vision. For example, if a small child was running across an open area, heading for the road, a motorist with limited peripheral vision may not see the child in time to react quickly.

2. **Tunnel vision** is an extremely restricted visual field, which can result in a narrow, circular vision that focuses only on one spot on the road. This usually occurs in people who are middle aged or older.

Colour blindness is also a common problem for many motorists, especially in determining the colour of traffic lights because certain colours, such as greens, browns, and reds, are the hardest to distinguish for those affected. Colour blind drivers will therefore at traffic lights recognise a change in brightness and know a change of lights by its position. Bright at the top identifies red.

There are other provisions that can be put in place to assist blind or partially-sighted pedestrians. These include:

- Textured paving at the edge of a footpath, which enables the pedestrian to feel a different surface under foot and recognise their position.
- Lowering of kerbs, to reduce the trip hazard at the edge of the footpath.
- The erection of railings to prevent the blind or partially-sighted person accidentally stepping out onto the road.
- A beeping repeater at traffic lights to alert the pedestrian that it is safe to cross.

It is very important that you visit the opticians if you suspect that your eyesight is deteriorating because you may need a pair of prescribed glasses. If you wear glasses or lenses you must only wear them in the conditions they are prescribed for, as they could also restrict or affect your vision if worn at any other time. If your vision seems more limited on bright days or at night you might find it helpful to wear tinted glasses or pull down your sun visor to block out sunlight and headlight glare.

Stress and depression

Driving while stressed or upset can affect your concentration, as your mind is not likely to be on your driving. You are more likely to make careless manoeuvres or mistakes if you are distracted, putting yourself and others at risk. Stress can make you impatient, increase aggression towards other motorists and affect your judgement. Running late, exam pressure, a busy day at work or reliving an argument are all likely to affect your focus and impair your reactions. For example, if you are stuck behind an elderly driver on a bad country road you may decide to risk overtaking if you are in a hurry.

Vulnerable road users

When driving on the roads you must always show consideration towards all other road users and pedestrians. Some people will be more vulnerable on the roads than others. The young, the elderly, the disabled and non-motorised road users are all more vulnerable on the road than vehicle drivers who are fit and able.

Age

As people get older their eyesight and hearing sometimes deteriorates, which can slow their reactions and impair their driving. Poor eyesight can lead to inaccurate manoeuvres, which could cause a collision. As a driver you should be patient with older drivers and give them as much time and room as possible – they have as much right to use the road as younger drivers.

Young children are not fully aware of the dangers associated with the road. When walking, adults should always keep children to the inside of the road or footpath in case they walk out in front of a vehicle. When driving, you should always reduce your speed if you see children playing nearby or walking on the road because their actions can be unpredictable. Similarly, you should slow down if you see a person with a pram, as the pram's extra width and length makes it more vulnerable. Someone may even try to cross between parked cars, pushing the pram slightly out onto the road to get a good view. People with prams should ideally cross at a designated crossing point, such as a zebra or light controlled crossing. However, if there is no crossing point nearby they should find an open space to cross, where they can clearly see the road in both directions and any traffic behind them.

Disability

Wheelchair users are limited by their chair's speed and movement when crossing the road. They will not be able to react as quickly as pedestrians on foot. Their chairs can also reduce their visibility, as they are quite low down, sometimes making crossing between parked cars dangerous. Similarly, people with leg or foot injuries will have similar speed and reaction problems, as they are limited by their walking aids. As a driver you must therefore look out, slow down and stop for people with mobility problems crossing the road.

Disabled drivers can find certain manoeuvres difficult in their vehicles, such as parking, changing gears or even getting out of their vehicle. As a driver you must be aware and considerate of disabled drivers to prevent collisions occurring. Some vehicles are specifically designed for disabled drivers. These are known as mobility vehicles. Alterations may include a hand-only operated braking system, button controls, a swivel seat to enable easy access and a dashboard lever-operated gear stick.

People who are blind or partially-sighted generally rely on sound, guide dogs or other people for assistance. This can make crossing the road quite difficult. Therefore you should always show consideration by slowing down and stopping to allow plenty of time for them to cross.

FOR YOUR FOLDER

1. Why are young children vulnerable on the roads?
2. How should a person with a pram cross a road were there are parked cars?
3. List two things that might affect an elderly person's driving skills.
4. If you see a blind or partially-sighted person crossing a road when you are driving what should you do?

THINK

1. Make a list of other non-motorised road users you think are disadvantaged on the road.
2. Think of three advantages non-motorised road users might have when on the roads.

Cycling

Cycling on the roads today requires your full attention and above all, awareness of other road users. Cyclists can be regarded as vulnerable road users because a safety framework, like that of vehicles, does not surround them. Therefore if you are cycling you must be aware of the movements of all the vehicles around you. It is also important that you carry out your manoeuvres safely and signal correctly to inform other motorists of your intentions. In towns and cities cycle lanes allow cyclists to cycle in safety whilst also helping to reduce congestion improving traffic flow. Weather conditions can also prove problematic to cyclists. Rain will leave the roads greasy and slippy, and strong winds or large vehicles passing at speed can cause a loss of balance. Children are especially at risk when riding a bicycle because they generally have less knowledge and experience of the road and its procedures than an adult.

It is essential that all cyclists wear the appropriate safety clothing and the three most important items are:

CYCLE HELMET
PADDED CLOTHING
FLUORESCENT CLOTHING

It is important to avoid wearing long coats and loose clothing when cycling because these could become tangled in the bicycle chain. Cyclists should never carry anything hanging from their handlebars as this may cause balance problems and affect the steering and control of the bicycle. On public roads cyclists should not cycle more than two abreast and should avoid cycling too close to the side of a road in case they clip a kerb with their pedal or lose control on a water gully cover. Children aged ten and above can take part in the National Cycling Proficiency Scheme (NCPS), which provides safety training in cycle riding. This scheme enables the young cyclist to gain knowledge and understanding of how to cycle safely on the roads.

In Northern Ireland all bicycles used on public roads are expected to have a white front light, a red rear light and a red rear reflector. Before taking a bicycle onto the roads you must make sure that your bicycle meets the following legal requirements:

LIGHTS AND REFLECTORS ARE CLEAN AND IN GOOD WORKING ORDER

TYRES ARE IN GOOD CONDITION AND AT THE CORRECT PRESSURE

BRAKES AND GEARS ARE WORKING CORRECTLY

FOR YOUR FOLDER

1. Why are cyclists regarded as vulnerable road users?
2. Why do weather conditions pose an extra threat to cyclists?
3. Why are children considered to be more at risk than adults on a bicycle?
4. How can children be educated in cycling safety?
5. Why is it important not to wear loose clothing or long coats while cycling?
6. Name three items of safety equipment that a cyclist should wear.

FOR YOUR FOLDER

7. Name five legal requirements that a bicycle must adhere to before taking to the roads.

Look at the 'Rules for cyclists' and 'You and your bicycle' sections in your *Highway Code* book. Answer the following questions in relation to these sections.

8. What must a bicycle have between sunset and sunrise?
9. State two advantages of cycle lanes.

Distractions for motorists

Road traffic collisions can occur very suddenly. A lack of concentration by a driver, rider or pedestrian may unfortunately lead to death or serious injury. You must learn to ignore everyday distractions when driving to enable you to concentrate fully on your driving and the road ahead.

Internal distractions

You must be aware of, and avoid creating, internal distractions before setting out on a journey. A number of distractions inside the vehicle that you may have to contend with are listed below:

- Fumbling with radio controls and not concentrating on the road ahead could force you to brake suddenly, sway or manoeuvre carelessly.
- Pets that are not properly secured, out of sight, could distract your attention and lead to careless driving.
- Children or objects not properly secured can also distract you if they are moving around inside the vehicle, are shouting or asking you questions.
- Attempting to read a map while driving could be very dangerous because you would not be concentrating on the road ahead.
- Using a mobile phone while driving leaves you only one hand free to drive with, reducing your control of the vehicle. Your concentration will also be on your conversation and not on the road in front of you.
- Trying to eat and drink while driving again leaves you only one hand free to drive with, reducing your control.

Any of these actions could lead to an unfortunate collision and some are even illegal.

Distractions for Motorists....

External distractions

In towns and cities there will be more external distractions that can impair your concentration when driving. A number of distractions outside the vehicle that you may have to contend with are listed below:

- Children playing along the side of a road or a ball bouncing in front of your vehicle will obviously distract your attention from the road ahead, which could force you to brake suddenly, swerve or manoeuvre carelessly.
- Pedestrians may walk out in front of your vehicle and you may have to brake or swerve suddenly.
- Dogs or animals on the loose may run out in front of your vehicle, again forcing you to brake or swerve.
- Advertisements on billboards may take a moment to read and divert your concentration from the road ahead. This could prevent you from braking in time if another vehicle in front of you slows down. You may also be slow to move off from a junction if you do not notice that the lights have changed, irritating other road users.
- Litter blowing may catch your eye and distract your attention from the road ahead.
- Other motorists' manoeuvres may distract you or cause you to hesitate as you try to figure out their intentions.
- Road traffic collisions can distract your attention from the road ahead as you look to see if there are any casualties or damage. Try to concentrate on the road in front of you in case you cause another collision.

 **THINK**

Think about the different forms of advertising on the roads. Explain how such advertising can distract drivers and the possible consequences of this distraction.

 FOR YOUR FOLDER

1. Name the two types of distractions that motorists have to contend with.
2. Make a list of some distractions inside a vehicle.
3. Make a list of some distractions outside a vehicle.
4. What consequences could there be for a motorist because of these distractions?
5. Explain why using a mobile phone while driving is dangerous for a motorist.
6. Why are road traffic collisions a distraction to motorists?

Speeding

Speeding is one of the most frequent causes of road collisions. Disregarding speed limits is more common among drivers under 25 years old than drivers over 25. Young drivers, often males, can be too confident and some take risks. As they are generally less experienced than older drivers, they often do not realise the dangers associated with speed and the need for increased stopping distances, particularly in the ever-changing road conditions. The government has introduced a number of measures to attempt to reduce such collisions. For example, warning signs inform motorists of the dangers on the road ahead. Traffic calming measures, such as those listed below, are also used to slow down motorists in residential or urban areas:

SPEED CUSHIONS
SPEED HUMPS
ROAD NARROWING
HORIZONTAL DEFLECTION
GATEWAYS

Penalty points can be issued if speed limits are not adhered to on public roads. Speed cameras have also been introduced to assist the police traffic branch in catching and penalising speeding motorists. These cameras can be permanent or temporary. Each type of road has a national speed limit that must be adhered to by motorists.

Motorists may, on occasion, have to drive at a speed that is lower than the recommended speed limit, for example when there is a hazard ahead, such as a collision or animals/children on the road.

On some roads crawler lanes have been introduced for larger, slow-moving vehicles, allowing motorists to pass safely without having to overtake on the wrong side of the road.

It is important to drive at a speed that allows you to stop well within the distance you can see to be clear in front of you.

Speed Limits	Built-up areas	Single carriage-ways	Dual carriage-ways	Motorways
Type of vehicle	mph (km/h)	mph (km/h)	mph (km/h)	mph (km/h)
Cars & motorcycles (including car-derived vans up to 2 tonnes maximum laden weight)	30 (48)	60 (96)	70 (112)	70 (112)
Cars towing caravans or trailers (including car-derived vans and motorcycles)	30 (48)	50 (80)	60 (96)	60 (96)
Buses, coaches and minibuses (not exceeding 12 metres in overall length)	30 (48)	50 (80)	60 (96)	70 (112)
Goods vehicles (not exceeding 7.5 tonnes maximum laden weight)	30 (48)	50 (80)	60 (96)	70[1] (112)
Goods vehicles (exceeding 7.5 tonnes maximum laden weight)	30 (48)	40 (64)	50 (80)	60 (96)

The safest rule is never to get closer than the combined overall thinking and braking distances. 'Tailgating' is a term used to describe vehicles that are driving to close to a vehicle in front.

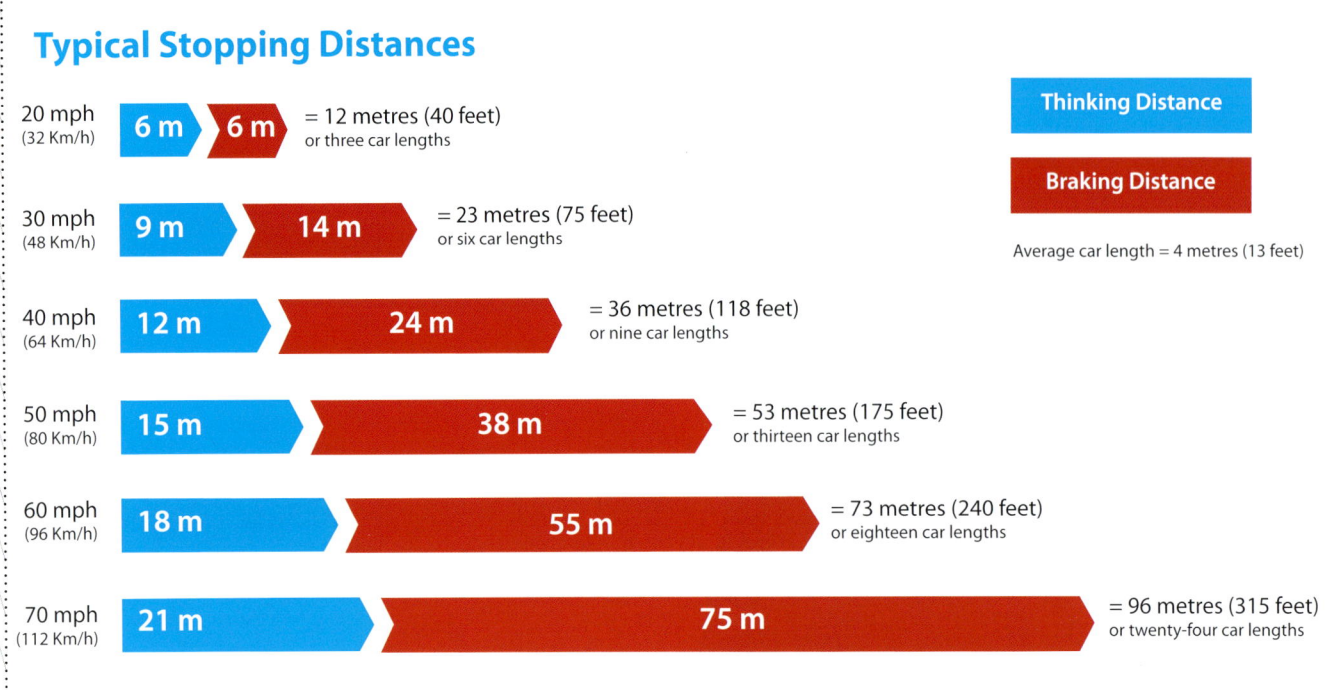

You have to be able to anticipate the need to stop and be aware of possible dangers. You must always apply common sense and use your judgement to assess different situations. In good conditions a two-second time gap is generally sufficient. This is often known as the 'two second rule'. This gap should be at least doubled on wet roads and increased even further on icy roads. Refer to your *Highway Code* book for further information.

FOR YOUR FOLDER

1. If you are caught speeding, name two possible consequences of this action.
2. Why do you think some young people drive much faster than older drivers?
3. Study the national speed limits and state the speed limits for the following:
   (a) Cars in built-up areas
   (b) Cars on a dual-carriageway
   (c) Coaches on a single-carriageway
   (d) Goods vehicles not exceeding 7.5 tonnes in built-up areas
   (e) Cars towing caravans on a motorway

FOR YOUR FOLDER

(f) Goods vehicles exceeding 7.5 tonnes on a single carriageway

4. How is the 'two second rule' useful to drivers?
5. When should the 'two second rule' be increased?
6. Suggest two reasons why a speed limit of 20 mph could be applied in a housing estate.
7. Name two ways in which road engineers can reduce vehicle speed on urban streets.
8. Suggest two reasons why speed limits are lower in towns than outside of towns.

Methods to reduce road traffic collisions

Three main methods are used to help reduce road collisions and these are commonly referred to as the three Es:

ENGINEERING
ENFORCEMENT
EDUCATION

Engineering

Engineering can be divided into two main areas:

1. Traffic engineering

Traffic engineering involves looking after and maintaining existing roads to ensure the safety of all road users. Maintenance includes upgrading safety measures on existing roads, such as the introduction of traffic calming measures and road surfaces. Traffic engineering also involves the designing and building of new roads, dual-carriageways and motorways. A number of factors must be considered to ensure essential safety measures are taken when designing a new road, some of which are listed below:

- Sharpness of curves/corners
- Gradients, hills, climbing lanes
- Footpaths
- Cycle tracks
- Drainage
- Parking provision
- Safety fencing

In Northern Ireland the DOE and some private firms work along with the Department For Regional Development to carry out this work.

2. Vehicle engineering

Vehicle engineering involves designing and manufacturing vehicles that will perform safely on the roads and provide as much protection as possible to all individuals within the vehicle. Two main elements need to be considered in designing and manufacturing vehicles.

- Primary safety
- Secondary safety

Primary safety involves the aspects that make a vehicle perform safely under everyday conditions, such as:

- effective lights
- effective wipers for good visibility
- adjustable seating and steering
- ABS (anti-lock brakes)
- good suspension and tyres
- good layout of controls

Secondary safety involves aspects that assist a vehicle when it is involved in a collision, such as:

- seat belts
- side impact bars
- collapsible steering column
- airbags
- head restraints to prevent whiplash
- padded dashboard and headlining
- shock absorbing bumpers
- burst-proof locks
- laminated glass
- crumple zones

Enforcement (The Law)

There are a large number of road traffic laws that cover the operation of motor vehicles. The most important of these laws are summarised in the *Highway Code* book, which provides information on all the correct road procedures. These laws address issues such as driving on the roads, drinking and driving, the use of both front and rear seat belts and parking restrictions. The police, DVA Enforcement Officers, parking attendants, and Customs and Excise Officers are mainly responsible for enforcing these laws. DVA Enforcement Officers concentrate on dealing with motorists that have not been taxed. Parking attendants are employed in towns and cities to issue parking tickets to vehicles parked in no-parking zones or otherwise illegally parked. They also check that vehicles parked in proper parking zones have paid the correct tariff for the waiting times. Customs and Excise Officers specialise in checking vehicles for the illegal use of fuel. For example, diesel vehicles are legally required to use white diesel, however, some motorists will buy the cheaper, red, agricultural diesel and hope that they will not be checked by customs.

Most police forces have a traffic division which specialises in road traffic offences, such as speeding and drink driving. In Northern Ireland there is a penalty points system in place whereby if a motorist receives twelve penalty points for traffic offences within a three-year period, the driver will automatically lose his or her license and be disqualified for a set period of time imposed by the courts. Remember that after passing your driving test, as a restricted driver you will have to resit your test if you receive six penalty points within your first two years' driving. Speeding, badly worn tyres, no seat belt, drink driving and careless driving are just some of the offences that will lead to a driver picking up penalty points. There are two types of offences:

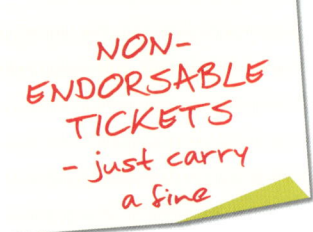

ENDORSABLE TICKETS – carry a fine and penalty points

NON-ENDORSABLE TICKETS – just carry a fine

Education

All road users have a responsibility to be aware of the safe and proper way to use the roads. Education starts in the home, where our parents constantly remind us about the dangers involved with using the roads. In primary schools this knowledge is reinforced by learning the **Green Cross Code**. Two important points highlighted in the Green Cross Code are:

1. Stop, Look and Listen
2. Cross from a safe place

Some primary schools also introduce their pupils to the National Cycling Proficiency Scheme (NCPS), usually in primary six or seven. This scheme teaches children how to cycle safely on the roads and makes them aware of possible dangers. Some secondary, grammar, comprehensive and high schools offer Motor Vehicle and Road User Studies (MVRUS) as a GCSE subject for one or two years at age fifteen and above. This course enables pupils to learn about all road laws, vehicle manoeuvres and traffic management as well as an element of practical moped riding. In a final attempt to educate all road users, from age 17 a computerised theory element based on the *Highway Code* book must be passed before taking the practical driving test. To ensure your own safety and the safety of others on the roads it is best to take driving lessons with a specialist instructor. By doing so you will learn all the correct procedures and manoeuvres properly and have the best possible chance of passing the practical driving test.

Educational Timeline

- Education starts in the home by our parents at an early age.
- Primary schools teach the Green Cross Code and NCPS.
- At years 11 and 12 a GCSE in MVRUS can be taught.
- From 17 years old a computerised theory test must be passed before taking the driving test.
- The **Department for Infrastructure (DFI)** continues to promote and educate road safety through various advertising campaigns.
- There are various initiatives on Road Safety in Northern Ireland. Some of them as follows:

Road Safe NI
www.roadsafeni.org

NI Road Safety Partnership
www.nidirect.gov.uk/articles/ni-road-safety-partnership

Share The Road To Zero
www.sharetheroadtozero.com

A number of publicity campaigns have been set up over the years to make the general public aware of the dangers of using public roads. Anti-drink-driving campaigns are probably the most publicised, especially in the lead up to the Christmas period. The consequences of speeding and not wearing your seat belt are often well documented in local media and adverts are often played on the radio, TV and posted on billboards. 'Be safe, be seen' is a campaign used to highlight the dangers of children coming home from school in the dark winter evenings. Reflective and fluorescent clothing and equipment has also been distributed to pupils in many schools.

FOR YOUR FOLDER

1. What are the three main approaches to collision prevention?
2. What two main areas is engineering split up into?
3. What does traffic engineering involve?
4. What does vehicle engineering involve?
5. What are the two main areas of vehicle engineering?
6. What aspects of a vehicle does primary safety look at?
7. What aspects of a vehicle does secondary safety look at?
8. What is enforcement?
9. Make a list of the different ways in which you can be educated in road safety.

THINK

Choose a recent road safety advertising campaign and research its aims and success on the Internet. Examples of recent DFI Road Safety adverts are:

- You Decide
- Friends Don't Distract Friends
- Never, Ever Drink and Drive
- What Are You Missing Out On?
- Be Bike Aware – Take Another Look

Seat belts

Wearing seat belts saves lives and reduces the risk of serious injury in a collision. The seat belt is an essential secondary safety item fitted inside vehicles and should always be put on before setting out on a journey. Seat belts are discussed in more detail in Chapter 2, on page 55.

Chapter Two

LEGAL REQUIREMENTS

MOTOR INSURANCE

Any motorist taking a vehicle out onto the roads must be insured to drive it. Motor insurance will provide you with financial protection if you are involved in a collision on the roads.

Types of insurance

There are different types of insurance cover and the following terminology is used to explain the various types of cover available:

First party/policy holder/proposer	This is any motorist with, or looking for, insurance.
Second party/broker	This is the insurance company or insurance company's representative selling the insurance.
Third party	This is any other person that becomes involved in a road traffic collision.
Premium	The price paid for insurance.
Policy	All the details of your insurance cover and the factors used to determine your premium.
Certificate	Legal proof of insurance.

Types of insurance...

Cover note	This is a temporary insurance certificate covering the driver for 30–60 days while a permanent hardcopy of the certificate is being drawn up.
Proposal form	A question form that the applicant fills in to outline the facts needed for the contract.
Underwriter	The person within the insurance company who is responsible for deciding whether or not to accept an insurance proposal based on the information provided by the road user.
Utmost good faith	Describes an individual that acted honestly with regard to an insurance claim.
Declined task/risk	An insurance company may not pay a claim if the road user has not honestly informed them of any important issues, such as the road user having a driving conviction. When seeking insurance the applicant is often asked if he or she has ever been declined before.
Indemnity	Compensation for loss or damage, restoring a person's financial position to what it was before the loss occurred.
Renewal notice	A reminder that your insurance for the year or six months is coming to an end, the details of the new start date and the amount to be paid for the following period.
Excess	This is the amount that you, as the owner, must pay for the damages if you have a collision and are at fault. Usually a fixed sum or percentage, this amount will be agreed by both the insurance company and yourself when the policy is being drawn up. The insurance company pays the remaining damage costs.
No claims bonus	Each year your insurance premium will be reduced if you do not claim from the insurance company. The percentage discount rises each year. From your sixth year the premium will not be reduced any further but remain at its lower price.
Protected bonus	This protects your no claims bonus. It will cost more to add this agreement to a policy.
Knock for knock	This is where an insurance company will only cover the damage costs to the vehicle they insure, regardless of who is at fault.
International Motor Insurance Card	This document is issued by your insurance company and is required if driving in any countries that are part of the European Union. It is now required for crossing the border from Northern Ireland to the Republic of Ireland.
Agent	Businesses looking to sell motor insurance.
Personal liability	Accepting responsibility for causing a road collision and what you are personally responsible for paying.

An insurance company might issue several documents to a motorist such as: renewal notice, policy, premium, certificate, cover note, green card.

There are three types of motor insurance:

1. Third party

This is a basic type of motor insurance that covers you if you damage the property of or injure a third party while you are driving. However, it does not cover you for any damage you cause to yourself or your vehicle.

2. Third party fire and theft

This type of insurance is exactly the same as third party, with the additional benefit that it also allows you to claim if your car is stolen or set on fire.

3. Fully comprehensive

This type of insurance covers all parties involved in a collision. It is the most expensive type of insurance because it provides the best protection. If you have comprehensive insurance you are also covered to drive another person's car, but only third party. If you are involved in a collision while driving someone else's vehicle you will have to pay for any damages caused to that vehicle. You can add an 'any driver clause' to your vehicle, guaranteeing that anyone with a valid driving licence is insured to drive your car. However, this will obviously cost more.

If you are considering driving someone else's vehicle on the road it is a good idea to check what you will be covered for with your insurance company.

FOR YOUR FOLDER

1. What does the term policy holder mean?
2. What does the term no claims bonus mean?
3. What is the difference between an insurance policy and an insurance certificate?

Factors affecting the cost of motor insurance

A number of factors affect the cost of motor insurance.

The driver

- Age
- Driving record (any previous claims, convictions or penalty points)
- Occupation
- Residence
- Type of cover

The vehicle

- Type and size
- Security (alarm)
- Parking location
- Type of insurance cover
- Other named drivers (especially those under 21 or over 65)
- Make of vehicle
- Performance
- Engine capacity
- Vehicle security
- Age of vehicle

When applying for insurance you will be asked various questions about these factors, allowing the insurance company to measure your level of risk. The company can then calculate the cost of insurance and provide a quote for either six months or one year. It is essential that you answer these questions honestly because if you provide the company with any false information they do not have to pay your claim if you are involved in a collision. It is in your best interests to try to truthfully convince insurance companies that you are a low-risk driver. The lower your risk, the less you will have to pay for insurance.

The age of a driver greatly influences insurance premiums. Young male drivers, aged between 17 and 24, will usually have to pay a high premium because insurance companies see them as the highest risk category. They are thought to be risk-takers, who drive too fast in cars that are too powerful for them to handle. Elderly drivers may also have to pay high insurance premiums because they are also considered to be high-risk candidates. This is because some elderly drivers have failing health, eyesight and hearing. Insurance companies believe this can slow their reactions and make them more likely to misjudge distances.

The road user's driving record is a crucial factor in determining an insurance premium. A 'no claims bonus' is a valuable asset. Each year your insurance premium will be reduced if you do not claim from the insurance company. It can decrease your premium by as much as 70% in your sixth year without claiming. After your sixth year it will not be reduced any further. A rough guide to the yearly discount is summarised in the table below:

Year	Percentage discount
1	30%
2	40%
3	50%
4	60%
5	65%
5 years + and over 50 years old	70%

Insurance companies will provide motorists who have accumulated several years of no claims bonus with an option, at an additional cost, to protect their no claims discount. This is known as a protected bonus.

FOR YOUR FOLDER

1. List the main factors that influence the cost of insurance.
2. Why is a driver's age an important factor in calculating the cost of insurance?
3. List the three main types of insurance.
4. Briefly explain what third party insurance covers.

FOR YOUR FOLDER

5. What type of insurance is the most expensive?
6. What is the purpose of a cover note?
7. What does the term 'indemnity' mean?
8. What does the term 'any driver clause' mean?

LEGAL DOCUMENTATION

All the details of your insurance cover and the factors used to determine your premium will be displayed and documented in your insurance policy. However, your most important document is your insurance certificate. This provides a brief summary of your cover and is the legal proof needed to tax your car or to present to the police upon request.

Other types of documentation are required to drive a car.

Driving Licence

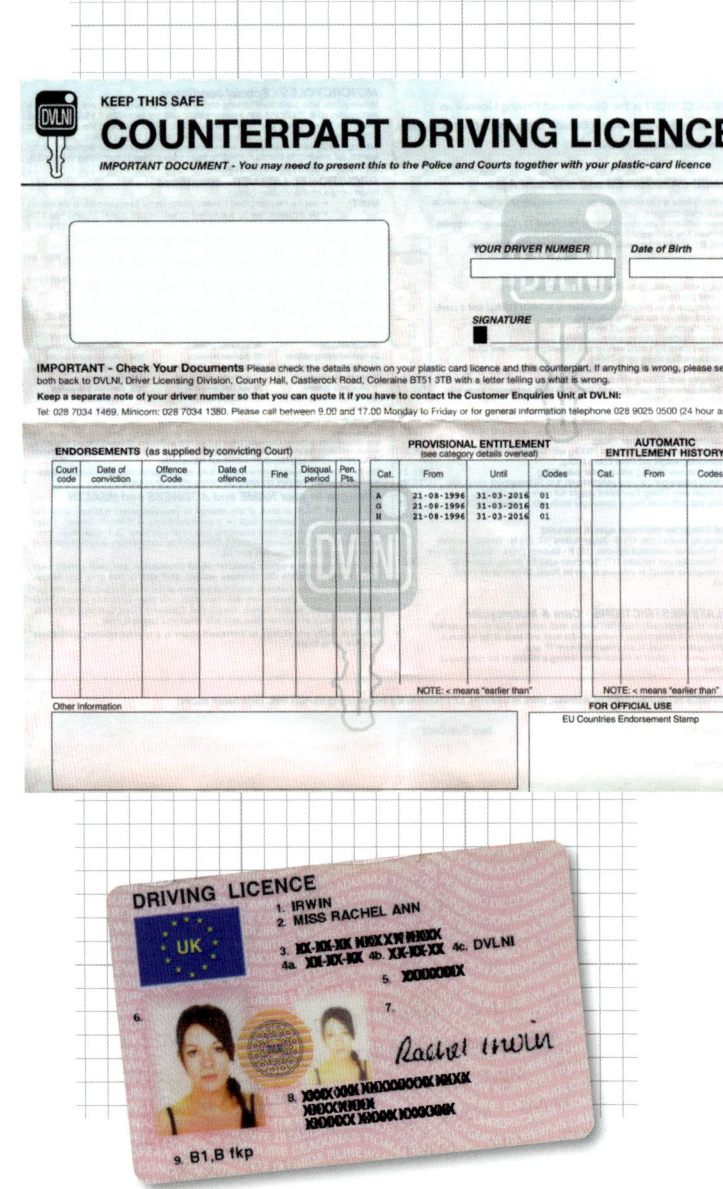

Upon reaching the age of 16 you can apply for your provisional driving licence. This licence allows you to drive agricultural vehicles and mopeds on the road, but no other vehicle until you reach 17. At 17 you can start learning to drive a car and can drive on the roads if accompanied by an adult aged 21 or over, who has held a full driving licence for three years or more. You must also be included on the vehicle's insurance and display 'L' plates. It is best to seek training from a specialist instructor when learning to drive, as it will improve your chances of passing the driving test, which you can sit from the age of 17.

On passing the driving test you will be issued with a driving licence consisting of two parts – a paper part and a card part. If the police, DVA (Driver and Vehicle Agency) or the courts request your licence you will need to provide both parts. The card is your actual licence and shows your full driving entitlements, including the types of vehicle the licence allows you to drive. The paper part shows other information, such as any endorsements (penalty points) on your licence. Penalty points can be given by a court if you are convicted of a driving offence.

The following information is found on a driving licence:
- name
- address
- date of birth
- date of issue
- date of expiry
- driving licence number
- signature of licence owner
- codes for the classes of vehicle the person is permitted to drive.

Newly qualified drivers in Northern Ireland must obey the following legal requirements:

1. Display 'R' plates for one year after passing their test.
2. Restrict their speed to 45 mph for one year after passing their test.

The restrictions above do not apply in England, Scotland and Wales. To drive an LGV (large goods vehicle), PSV (public service vehicle) or PCV (passenger carrying vehicle), you must be at least 21 years old, hold a full driving licence and sit a specialist driving test.

If you obtain 6 penalty points in your first two years of driving you will lose your licence and have to re-sit the driving test.

FOR YOUR FOLDER

1. At what age can you apply for your provisional licence?
2. At what age can you drive a moped on the road?
3. Name two legal requirements for newly qualified drivers.
4. How long does a driver have to display 'R' plates for?
5. What happens if a newly qualified driver obtains six penalty points in his or her first two years of driving?
6. What do LGV, PSV and PCV stand for?
7. What age must you be to drive an LGV vehicle?

Vehicle Excise Duty (VED)

Vehicle Excise Duty (VED) is a tax paid on every vehicle using public roads. VED is paid and renewed every 6 or 12 months depending on which option is more affordable for the road user at the time of expiry. A reminder is sent out to the registered keeper prior to expiry reminding them that it is time to renew. The process of renewing is typically carried out online by the vehicle owner.

Drivers of new and relatively fuel-efficient vehicles pay a lower rate of vehicle excise duty than those who own older, less fuel-efficient vehicles. All vehicles fall into a certain VED band depending on their CO_2 emissions and this band determines how much the vehicle owner will have to pay. Vehicle manufacturers are therefore striving to manufacture cleaner, less-polluting vehicles to meet environmental targets set by the government to help reduce global warming.

Electric vehicles were initially exempt from VED but from 2025 owners of electric vehicles are expected to pay VED using a new banding system.

A **SORN** (Statutory Off Road Notification) document can be obtained to declare ownership of a vehicle that is officially 'off the road' and where it will be staying. You will not have to pay VED for this vehicle as you will not be driving it on the roads. A SORN vehicle does not require an MOT.

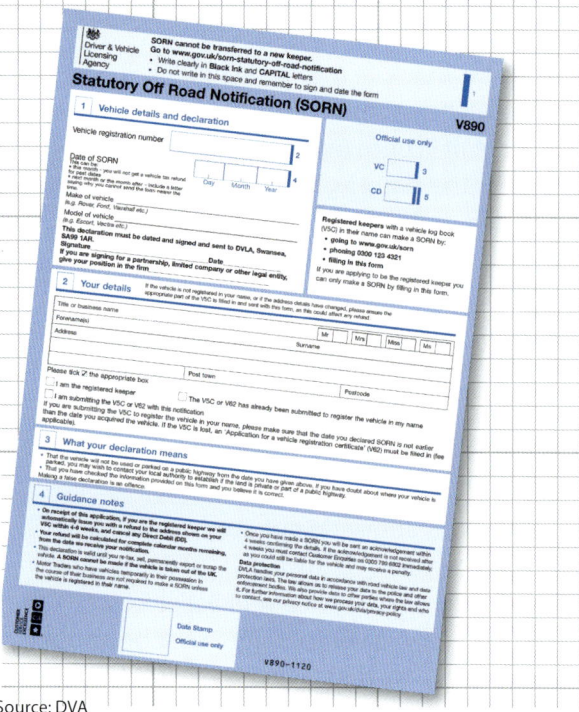

Source: DVA

FOR YOUR FOLDER

1. What is vehicle excise duty?
2. How do you pay for a vehicle excise duty?
3. How is VED calculated?
4. What is a SORN document?

Tax Book
(V5 Vehicle Registration Document)

This document is not proof of ownership but it shows who is responsible for registering the vehicle and paying its VED. The V5 lists a vehicle's make, model, colour, date of registration, chassis number, VED band and its previous owners. This form is also used to declare any changes or modifications to the vehicle to the DVLA and has a section to be completed when selling or exporting the vehicle. When the DVLA receive this form as notification that you have sold a vehicle they will automatically end the Vehicle Excise Duty and make a refund to the registered keeper for any outstanding months that have already been paid for.

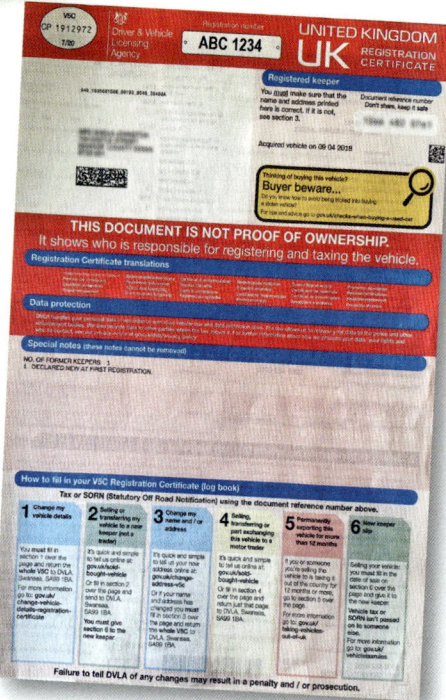

Source: DVLA

MOT
(Vehicle test certificate)

All vehicles older than four years old in Northern Ireland must complete an annual MOT test at a government-controlled DVA centre. In England all vehicles older than three years old must complete an annual MOT test, which is carried out by designated garages. A vehicle is awarded an MOT certificate as proof that it is in a good condition and safe to drive on the roads. This legal requirement encourages road users to look after their vehicle, ensuring it has had regular maintenance and safety checks by a qualified mechanic. The MOT test is only carried out once per year and therefore only assesses the vehicle's condition at that time. However, it is a comprehensive inspection which helps to improve the roadworthiness of older vehicles.

Before taking your vehicle for its MOT test it is wise to have it serviced or checked by a mechanic and to wash it (if the underside of your vehicle is too dirty they will not test it). These steps will give your vehicle the best possible chance of passing the test, saving you the cost of a re-test just because your vehicle needed something small fixed. The main checks carried out during the MOT test are the following:

- seat belts
- brakes
- electrics (lights, wipers, horn, indicators)
- steering and suspension systems
- tyres
- exhaust system (including its carbon monoxide and hydrocarbon emissions)

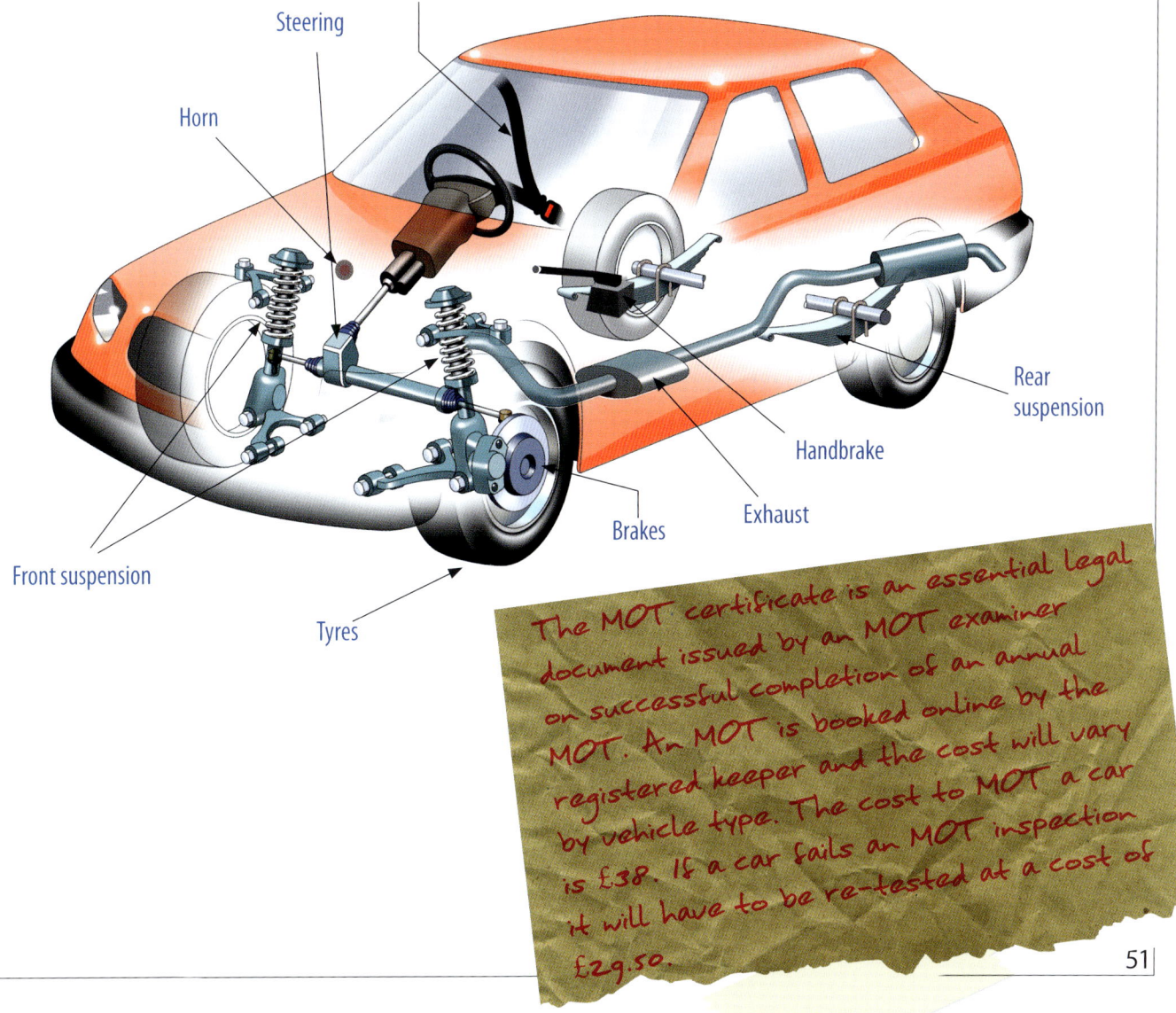

The MOT certificate is an essential legal document issued by an MOT examiner on successful completion of an annual MOT. An MOT is booked online by the registered keeper and the cost will vary by vehicle type. The cost to MOT a car is £38. If a car fails an MOT inspection it will have to be re-tested at a cost of £29.50.

FOR YOUR FOLDER

1. What is a vehicle registration document and what details does it provide?
2. What are vehicles over four years of age legally required to have and why?
3. What two things could a vehicle owner do to prepare a car for the MOT?
4. Make a list of checks carried out during the MOT.
5. What are the names of the two exhaust gases that are checked?
6. What happens if a vehicle does not pass all the checks?

THINK

Draw a table similar to the one below. Using the Internet research each of the legal requirements associated with driving. Use this information to fill in the spaces in the table.

Legal requirements	Cost
Vehicle Excise Duty ('road tax') (per year)	
MOT (per year)	
Provisional driving licence **Full driving licence** **Theory test** **Practical test**	
Insurance (average motor insurance for a 17 year old per year)	
Total cost of driving (in first year)	

THE VEHICLE

It is important that all vehicles' operating systems are checked before they are taken onto the road to ensure that they are working correctly. The windscreen wipers must function properly to keep the windscreen clear, assisting visibility. Legal requirements insist that windscreen washers always have fluid in them to clear the windscreen with water or screen wash if it gets dirty. Wiper blades are made of rubber, and will become worn and need replaced eventually. It is essential that your vehicle's horn is working in case you need to make people aware of your presence.

For example, if a reversing driver does not seem to see you, you could sound your horn to warn them that they are too close to your vehicle.

Vehicle lighting both improves your vision and allows other road users to see you, especially at night or in poor weather conditions. All lights, both front and rear, including brake lights and indicators, should be checked regularly in case a bulb has blown. Brake lights are essential for letting other motorists know that you are braking. If they are not working properly someone could drive into the back of your vehicle because they do not realise that you are slowing down. Indicators are similarly important because they inform other road users of your intentions.

Efficient brakes allow vehicles to slow down and stop safely. Brake pads generate heat by friction and will eventually wear away because of the constant rubbing against a brake disc or drum. Worn brake pads will make the braking system less efficient, which is dangerous because it will increase stopping distances. Therefore, brake pads will need replacing and should be checked at each service by your mechanic. It is also essential that a vehicle's steering is working efficiently to ensure the vehicle travels where you want it to. Wheels that are knocked out of alignment by striking something hard or uneven, such as a pothole or kerb, may cause a vehicle to pull to one side and affect its steering. If you feel the steering pulling to one side you should go to tyre service station to check the balance and alignment of your wheels.

Tyres

Good tyres are essential for the safe motoring of any vehicle and they should be checked regularly to ensure that.

- There are no foreign bodies such as nails, stones, thorns or glass stuck in the tyre treads or walls.
- All tyres are the correct tyre pressure. Tyres that are soft (with too little air in them) will make steering more difficult. Tyres that are hard (with too much air in them) can reduce grip with the road surface, making the car bounce. If a hard tyre strikes an object or hump when travelling on an uneven road surface it could puncture or 'blow out'.
- All tyres should be the same pressure to ensure the vehicle is well-balanced.
- The tyre treads should be clearly visible. As tyre treads are used to improve grip with the road surface and disperse surface water, it is essential that their depth is sufficient. You can check the tread depth by looking at a depth indicator on the tyre. If the indicator is still visible the tyre's

remaining tread depth is adequate. If it is worn away the tyre needs replaced.

The police sometimes check vehicles' tyre conditions at checkpoints. If any of the tyre pressures or tread depth are insufficient the vehicle's driver could receive a fine or penalty points.

The size of a tyre is sometimes printed on the side wall of a new tyre with information similar to this: 225/40 R18. This means that the tyre has a width of 225 mm, a profile of 40% and fits a rim or alloy with an 18 inch diameter.

The legal tread depth for cars, vans and light vehicles is 1.6 mm.

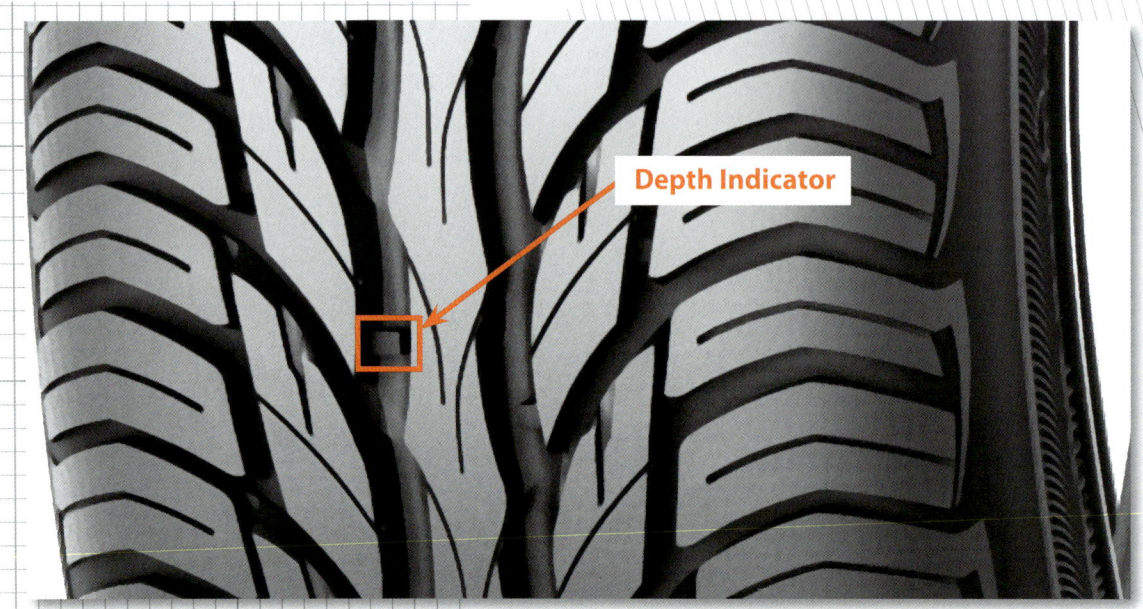

Depth Indicator

The legal tread depth for a motorcycle is 1.0 mm.

FOR YOUR FOLDER

1. Name three tyre checks that should be carried out regularly.
2. What effect will driving with soft tyres have on handling a vehicle?
3. What is the purpose of depth indicators on the tyres?
4. What is the legal tyre tread depth for a car?
5. What is the legal tyre tread depth for a motorcycle?

Seat Belts

You **must** always wear a seat belt if one is available, unless you are exempt. You may be exempt if you have a shoulder, chest or arm injury. Your doctor, GP or local hospital can provide a medical exemption certificate, which must be produced by the driver to the police if stopped. If you are stopped by the police and found not to be wearing a seat belt, you or the driver (if not yourself) are likely to receive penalty points or a fine. Adults should be responsible and set a good example to children by always putting on their seat belt. All children should be secured during travel using one of the following child restraints:

- Baby carrier
- Child seat
- Harness or booster seat

It is essential that the front passenger airbag is switched off if a vehicle is carrying a rear-facing baby seat in the front seat. If the vehicle was involved in a collision the child's head would be too close to the airbag, risking severe injury or death if it was activated.

You should look at the section on seat belts and child restraints more closely in your Highway Code book.

Summary of the legal requirements

	FRONT SEAT	REAR SEAT	WHO IS RESPONSIBLE?
Driver	Seat belt must be worn		Driver
Child under 3 years of age	Child restraint must be worn	Child restraint must be worn	Driver
Child aged 3–12 or under 1.35 metres	Child restraint must be worn	Child restraint must be worn	Driver
Child aged 12–13 or under 1.35 metres	Adult seat belt must be worn	Adult seat belt must be worn	Driver
Passenger aged 14 years and over	Seat belt must be worn	Seat belt must be worn	Passenger

FOR YOUR FOLDER

1. State two advantages of wearing seat belts.
2. Who is exempt from wearing seat belts?
3. What are the legal requirements for wearing seat belts in your *Highway Code* book?
4. What are the legal requirements regarding seat belts for children under the age of three?
5. What is considered an appropriate child restraint?

THINK

Using the Internet see if you can find any statistics relating to the regulations about the wearing of seat belts and note them under the following headings:

- Legal requirements
- Collision statistics
- Penalties imposed

MOTORCYCLE HELMETS

There are two main types of motorcycle helmets but they come in various shapes and sizes.

Both these types of helmets are made using the injection moulding process with high-impact-resistant plastic materials. Some helmets are designed with an aerodynamic shape. The inside of the helmets are lined with light padded foam that has a replaceable and washable sponge lining. Most helmets are manufactured with a good ventilation system that helps reduce fogging or steaming up. It also makes the helmets more comfortable to wear. The visor or shield is usually produced with an anti-scratch, anti-fog, high optic material to try and maintain good vision for motorists. All products manufactured can be sent to the British Standards Institute, where they are tested for quality, comfort and safety. Approved products will receive a recognisable, stamped, certification mark to show customers that the product is of a high quality and has been rigorously tested under operating conditions.

1. **Jet style/open faced**
   With these types of helmets the motorist's face is uncovered and the visor at the front can be removed.

FOR YOUR FOLDER

1. What are the two main types of motorcycle helmet?
2. Describe what a jet style helmet looks like.
3. Describe what a full face helmet looks like.

2. **Full face**
   With these helmets the motorist's face is covered. This can reduce the motorcyclist's visibility.

Chapter Three

ROAD TRANSPORT AND ITS EFFECT ON SOCIETY

TYPES OF TRANSPORT

TRANSPORT	ADVANTAGES	DISADVANTAGES
Car	Convenience; independence; good weather protection; quiet and comfortable; plenty of passenger room; various body styles; safer than travelling by bicycle or by motorcycle as the framework of a vehicle is designed to protect its occupants.	Expensive to purchase; expensive running costs; cannot drive until 17 years old; parking problems; restricted in heavy traffic; body corrosion; maintenance.
Motorcycle	Independence; cheaper to purchase and run than a car; can ride from 16 years old; easy to park; easy to manoeuvre in traffic.	Special clothing required; poor weather protection; high collision rate; poor protection if involved in a collision; difficult to control in adverse weather conditions; limited visibility in rain; only carries one or two passengers; all mechanics and electrics exposed to the weather and vandals when parked.
Bus	Generally plenty of passenger room; comfortable; relaxing; passengers do not have to think about parking; bus lanes means traffic can often be avoided; reduces congestion if more people use public transport; better for the environment if the number of vehicles used is reduced (lowers noise and air pollution); safer than travelling by car because of its larger framework, weight and size, allowing it to withstand greater impacts.	Restricted by bus timetable; cost per ride; can be quite full leaving little passenger room; passengers have to get themselves to and from the station/bus stop; may not be a bus stop near passengers' work/home/destination.

TRANSPORT	ADVANTAGES	DISADVANTAGES
Train 	Generally plenty of passenger room; comfortable; can get up and walk about; relaxing; do not have to think about parking; avoid traffic; safer than travelling by car because it travels on its own track and does not come into contact with other vehicles; its larger framework, weight and size also allow it to withstand greater impacts.	Restricted by train timetable; cost per ride (more than a bus); can be quite full leaving little passenger room; passengers have to get themselves to and from the station; may not be a station near passengers' work/home/destination.

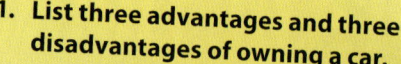

FOR YOUR FOLDER

1. List three advantages and three disadvantages of owning a car.
2. Suggest three types of public transport.
3. List two advantages and two disadvantages of travelling by bus.
4. State one main advantage of a bus lane in towns and cities.
5. Why is driving a motorcycle considered to be more dangerous than driving a motor car?

DEVELOPMENT OF TRANSPORT

Before the introduction of motor vehicles in the nineteenth century people still needed to travel. In the seventeenth and eighteenth centuries stagecoaches pulled by horses were used to carry passengers, and wagons pulled by horses were used to deliver materials and supplies.

In the nineteenth century the development of railways saw the first real alternative to horse-drawn vehicles – trains. Trains were popular as they were fast and carried larger numbers of passengers, materials and supplies. Bicycles were also very popular in the nineteenth century, as they enabled people to travel short distances independently. People travelling long distances to work often used bicycles to get to the nearest railway station. However, while the railway network was expanding another mode of power and transport was being developed.

In 1826 the first gas internal combustion road engine was developed. The new road vehicles that used this engine were very popular with the public but not with stagecoach or railway firms, which were losing custom. Local government officials were pressurised to impose higher road tax on steam-powered vehicles. They also introduced the 1865 Highways and Locomotives Act (the Red Flag Act). This act restricted the speed of steam-powered vehicles and a person had to walk in front of each vehicle carrying a red flag to warn other road users.

Development of the motor car

The biggest development in road travel came in 1885 when a German man called Karl Benz produced the first motor car, using an internal combustion engine to run on petrol. With the development of the motor car the law was forced to change and the 1865 Red Flag Act was replaced with The Locomotives on Highways Act 1896. This act set a new speed limit of 14 mph and forced all vehicles to carry a bell or other instrument to warn others of their approach.

BENZ PATENT MOTORWAGEN, 1885

Different shapes and makes of motor cars were developed over the years but in 1913 a man called Henry Ford introduced the assembly line. Before this, building a single motor car was both expensive and time-consuming. The assembly line meant that Ford could mass-produce his motor vehicle, the Ford Model T, as each individual vehicle could be assembled in an hour and a half.

FORD MODEL T ASSEMBLY LINE, 1913

Throughout the twentieth century the design and manufacture of motor vehicles gradually improved, with the introduction of hydraulic brakes, safety glass, bumpers and electric components such as lights, windscreen wipers, speedometers, radios and the horn. Manufacturers today continue to make improvements in the safety, design, technology and comfort of their vehicles to meet the ever-increasing demands of the consumer.

Over the past decade, hybrid and electric vehicles have become more common and popular. A **hybrid** vehicle uses both a conventional fuel-driven engine (petrol or diesel) and electric. The driver can switch between these engines depending on the driving scenario. For example, when the vehicle is at a low speed or sitting idling it could be switched to electric. For higher speeds and for more power it could be switched back to conventional fuel. These switches help the overall fuel efficiency of the vehicle.

One of the biggest advantages of the hybrid is that it runs more cleanly, making it more environmentally friendly. This reduces the owner's dependence on fossil fuels and lowers the impact of carbon emissions on the environment. Reduced Vehicle Excise Duty on hybrid vehicles also makes them cheaper to tax. The engine in a hybrid vehicle is also much smaller, making it lighter which helps to save energy. Its modern regenerative braking system means that each time the brake is applied the battery is recharged a little, which increases the time before the vehicle needs to stop and recharge. Another major advantages of hybrid vehicles is that they depreciate more slowly than pure petrol cars, and have a higher resale price.

Seventeenth century	(1600–1700)	Dust tracks were used by horses and stage coaches.
Eighteenth century	(1700–1800)	New roads were developed with more freedom for horses and stage coaches.
Nineteenth century	(1800–1900)	Railways, steam engines and bicycles were new attractions. The development of the first internal combustion engine. The first motor car was designed by Karl Benz in 1885.
Twentieth century	(1900–2000)	New roads are built to accommodate the development of the motor car. The assembly line and mass production of one vehicle was introduced by Henry Ford. The first motorways were built in the 1950s.
Twenty-first century	(2000–present)	The development of the modern-day motor car with improved technology, comfort and safety features.
	(2000–present)	The hybrid vehicle can be either petrol or diesel and can be switched from these fossil fuels to electric, making it more environmentally friendly.
	(2000–present)	Electric vehicles are very expensive but produce no greenhouse gases. This is seen as the future of motoring.

However, there are some disadvantages of hybrid vehicles such as the following:

- They can have less power than a pure petrol car.
- They are more expensive to purchase.
- They tend to have higher maintenance costs.
- The availability of charging stations.
- Battery replacement, if required, is expensive.

Electric vehicles are also better for the environment because they do not run on fossil fuels at all. No exhaust fumes are produced which improves air quality and helps to reduce greenhouse gases. Electric cars cost less money to maintain as the engines are much simpler, mechanically speaking, than petrol cars. This means that they do not require many of the fuel component replacements needed in petrol cars, and will not be subject to the same wear and tear of moving parts associated with petrol- or diesel-powered cars.

Electric cars are extremely quiet which reduces noise pollution, but this can also be a disadvantage as it is more difficult to hear an electric car approaching. This is particularly dangerous for pedestrians as they may not hear an electric vehicle coming and could step out in front of it.

The lack of availability of charging stations remains a problem in certain areas of Northern Ireland but efforts are being made to address this. Therefore, before setting out on a long journey, drivers of electric cars need to have their vehicle fully charged and plan their route to incorporate charging stops into their journey.

In summary, some of the advantages and disadvantages of electric vehicles are as follows:

Advantages

- No emissions at the point of use.
- Extremely quiet, reducing noise pollution.
- Can be charged at home, though this is more of a challenge for those without off-street parking.
- They often outperform petrol and diesel cars.
- Electric vehicles are seen as the future by government, with petrol and diesel cars to be phased out.
- Higher resale value.
- Cheaper to maintain over time.
- Free parking incentives.

Disadvantages

- Lack of availability of charging stations.
- Quiet nature makes it harder to hear them approaching.
- They can be less powerful, for example when towing.
- Expensive to purchase.

The relationship between collision prevention and motor vehicle technology

The vehicle industry is very competitive, with manufacturers mass-producing their products to keep costs as low as possible. Many factors influence the buyer's choice of vehicle including its type, cost, interior design and comfort. However, in all areas of vehicle design and manufacture, it is the safety of its occupants and its performance under everyday driving conditions that are given the most attention. The link between collision prevention and motor vehicle technology is a major factor influencing the design of motor vehicles. Car manufacturers are constantly improving and updating their primary and secondary safety features, because safety ratings are high on many consumers' wish lists.

primary safety

Primary safety relates to all the features that help a vehicle perform safely in everyday driving conditions. Some examples are:

- steering and location of the controls
- tyres
- lights and indicators
- effective wipers
- suspension

secondary safety

Secondary safety relates to all the features that protect a vehicle's occupants if it is involved in a road traffic collision. Some examples are:

- airbags
- seat belts
- side impact bars (to strengthen the door panels)
- crumple zones
- collapsible steering column
- laminated glass

These features were described in greater detail in the section entitled 'Methods to reduce traffic collisions' on page 41.

FOR YOUR FOLDER

1. Who designed the first motor car?
2. Draw a block diagram to show how transport has developed over the years.
3. Why do car manufacturers mass-produce their vehicles?
4. What is meant by the term primary safety?
5. List four items of primary safety on a motor vehicle.
6. What is meant by the term secondary safety?
7. List three items of secondary safety on a motor vehicle.

DEVELOPMENT OF THE MODERN ROAD SYSTEM AND TRAFFIC MANAGEMENT

Over 8000 years ago a typical road was simply a dust or dirt track made by people and horses. The introduction of stagecoaches meant that these tracks needed to be widened and flattened to allow the coaches to travel more smoothly. Roads needed constant updating and improving as road traffic increased. It became necessary to build longer-lasting roads, with smooth, waterproof surfaces. The introduction of tarmac in 1845 helped to achieve these smooth, waterproof roads. Roads today are built on foundations of concrete and stone, sometimes reinforced with steel mesh to prevent the concrete cracking under the weight of constant traffic. These foundations are coated with tarmac and laid with a slight incline from the centre to the edge of the road, allowing rain water to run into drains situated at the edge. With the ever-increasing population and advancements in technology, the conditions of roads are continually improving. Today there are a number of different types of roads:

Motorways – These are fast-moving roads that usually link major cities. They have a number of traffic lanes heading in each direction, with a central barrier or reservation separating the opposing directions. The signs on these roads generally have white lettering on a blue background and the speed limit is usually 70 mph, unless stated differently. The first motorways in the UK were designed and built in the 1950s to help ease traffic flow and to enable motorists to get to their destination quickly and safely. Learner drivers and agricultural vehicles are not allowed to use motorways because of their speed restrictions. Stopping and U-turns are also prohibited, and slip roads are used to enter and exit motorways, allowing traffic to remain travelling at, or to get up to, the required speed.

Dual-carriageways – These are also fast moving roads that link major towns and cities. These roads usually have two traffic lanes heading in each direction, also separated by a central reservation. The right-hand lane is used for fast moving traffic and overtaking. The speed limit is 70 mph unless signs state otherwise.

Single-carriageways – These roads can also be fast moving and are characterised by having no central reservation to separate the lanes of traffic travelling in opposite directions. The speed limit in rural areas is usually 60 mph.

Primary routes – These are used to describe major roads, and can include all types of carriageways. Except on motorways, primary routes have green signs with white letters.

Non-primary routes – These are ordinary town (urban) or country (rural) roads on which we generally drive most frequently. This type of road has signs with black lettering on a white background.

Single track roads – These are roads with only one traffic lane. If vehicles meet on this type of road one of the vehicles will have to pull into a gap and stop to allow the other to pass. If no gap is available at the meeting place one vehicle will have to reverse back along the road until it reaches a space wide enough to allow the other vehicle to pass.

Autostrada – This is the name given to motorways in Italy. The recommended speed limit on these motorways is 130 km/h (80 mph).

Autobahns – This is the name given to motorways in Germany. The first autobahns were built in the 1930s. The recommended speed limit on these motorways is 130 km/h (80 mph) and all signs are blue with white lettering.

Unfortunately, the upgrading and building of better roads usually encourages more vehicles onto the roads and faster speeds. Traffic congestion is also a common problem in towns, cities and built-up areas. A number

German Autobahn

of important road safety measures have been developed to ease traffic congestion and keep it flowing. The introduction of parking restrictions and one-way streets in towns and cities have been welcome additions for many motorists. Parking in towns and cities is monitored by parking attendants with many areas requiring a payment. Parking in towns and cities has also been eased by the creation of multi-storey car parks and park-and-ride systems that enable motorists to park outside the cities, reducing traffic congestion and pollution.

Pedestrian movement in cities has been eased by the introduction of pedestrian zones, wider pavements, narrower roads for vehicles, reduced speed limits and zebra crossings or signalised crossings. Usually, the only vehicles allowed into these zones are service vehicles, such as bin lorries, or those needed for carrying out repairs to shop fronts, footpaths etc. Sometimes delivery vehicles require close access to certain premises. These are often restricted to times are before or after the normal working hours of 8 am to 6 pm.

> Traffic calming measures are an essential environmental factor used to reduce speeding in built-up areas. These are described in greater detail in the section entitled 'Methods to reduce traffic collisions' on page 41 and in your Highway Code book.

speed humps

speed cushions

FOR YOUR FOLDER

1. How would you describe a typical road 8000 years ago?
2. What type of transport used these roads?
3. When were the first motorways built?
4. What colours are the signs and lettering on motorways?
5. What is a central reservation?
6. What does the term 'autostrada' mean?
7. What is meant by the term 'traffic calming'?
8. Name three traffic calming measures.
9. State two advantages of a pedestrianisation zone.
10. At what times are delivery vehicles and bin lorries usually allowed into a pedestrianised zone?
11. What is an autobahn?

horizontal deflection

SOCIAL AND ENVIRONMENTAL EFFECTS OF POLLUTION

All roads form part of the landscape and the environment, and all of us benefit from them as drivers, passengers, pedestrians or cyclists. The majority of homes have at least one car, if not two. This has an immediate impact on the environment. As the population increases so does the number of vehicles on our roads. Larger volumes of traffic will pollute the air that we breathe and increase noise levels. Increased noise levels can damage people's hearing or disturb people who live close to, or are in hospitals near, busy roads. However, there is a need for good road networks that cater for the large volume of traffic on the roads today.

Unfortunately, the need for new roads can sometimes have impacts on the landscape and countryside. Sometimes there is no practical alternative for a proposed road. This can often lead to conflict between land owners, local agencies or businesses who will lose land or business as a result of a new road. A new road may redirect traffic away from certain locations or communities, causing a loss of revenue to filling stations or roadside café's. However, if private lands or grounds are needed for new roads, compensation will be paid to the owners. Many new roads are unfortunately forced to carry traffic through:

- Valued landscapes
- Wildlife habitats and reserves
- Close to historic towns or occasionally sites of scientific and archaeological interest.
- Agricultural land
- Private property – gardens, farm yards, business yards, etc

Before a new road is designed, an environmental assessment is carried out to see what effects it could have on people and their environment. The assessment includes:

- The effect of traffic noise
- The effect on agriculture
- The effect on community severance (destruction of services and amenities)
- The effect of air pollution
- The visual impact
- The effect on heritage and conservation areas
- The effect on wildfowl and wildlife
- The effect on pedestrians and cyclists
- The disruption due to construction works
- The views from the road

Environmental experts have developed a number of ways to minimise the destruction of, and disruption to, the environment and the landscape. A few of these are as follows:

- Planting trees and certain seeding flowers that provide both food and cover for birds and small mammals.
- Cutting or lowering roads so that the countryside and visual impact of the landscape is less affected.
- Constructing or replacing natural features to maintain a pleasing appearance.

The Broadway underpass on the M1 in south Belfast.

- Building tunnels or underpasses for pedestrians and minor roads.
- Constructing underground tunnels or underpasses to help animals crossing busy roads, and placing nesting boxes under bridges and near road verges.

This wildlife underpass in LA county, USA, was constructed to allow animals such as bobcats, coyotes and American badgers to safely cross Harbour Boulevard. Harbour Boulevard is a four-lane road cutting through land managed by Puente Hills Landfill Native Habitat Preservation Authority.

FOR YOUR FOLDER

1. List three environmental factors that influence the design of a new road.
2. List three ways in which environmental experts can minimise the destruction to the environment.
3. How can animals be helped to cross the road?
4. List one example of how a new road has changed the environment in some way near your home.
5. How can the building of new roads affect air pollution?
6. Why is it important to plant new trees and replace as many natural features as possible when building new roads?

Effects of pollution

Traffic volumes in our society today have are major cause of increased levels of pollution. Exposure to air pollution can cause premature death and illnesses. There are a number of different types of exhaust pollutants:

- **Carbon monoxide** is a type of gas in the atmosphere that, when inhaled, restricts the flow of oxygen around the body. This affects the central nervous system, impairing physical co-ordination, vision and judgement.
- **Nitrogen oxides** are formed during the burning of petrol in the engine. These gases can cause breathing problems such as bad coughs, runny noses and sore throats.
- **Carbon dioxide** is a major greenhouse gas that seriously effects climate change.
- **Hydrocarbons** are emitted from vehicle exhausts as unburned fuel. These gases can cause coughing, sneezing, lung and eye irritation.
- **Sulphur dioxide** is a gas emitted from a vehicle's exhaust after diesel fuel has been burned. The buildup of this gas in the atmosphere causes acid rain. The air after a shower of rain still contains particles of sulphur, which can affect breathing and cause lung problems.
- **Lead** is a dangerous exhaust pollutant that can cause serious damage to the kidneys, liver and reproductive organs. It has been shown to contribute to behavioural problems and impair people's concentration.

Noise pollution from vehicles is often overlooked, but it is a real concern in many situations. Heavy traffic, traffic queues, sports exhausts, faulty exhausts, 'spinning the wheels', 'donuts', thumping music from stereos and vehicle horns are all forms of traffic noise. Some of it can easily be avoided if due care and consideration is given to communities and residents. Similarly, when road designers and engineers are building a new road they often incorporate a number of measures into their designs to reduce the effects of traffic noise, especially if the road is passing a residential area. These measures might include erecting fences and earth banks, and the planting of trees and bushes to soften the noise.

Efforts to reduce pollution

In an attempt to reduce exhaust gases, car manufacturers have fitted all modern vehicles with catalytic converters. These converters are used to remove carbon monoxide, hydrocarbons and nitrogen oxides from exhaust gases. Governments across the world require all vehicle manufacturers to insert catalytic converters into all vehicles to improve air quality and reduce the amount of harmful gases released into the atmosphere. These gases affect the environment, wildlife, cause climate change, and have led to an increase in the number of human health problems, such as respiratory breathing problems that affect the lungs and increase the risk of asthma.

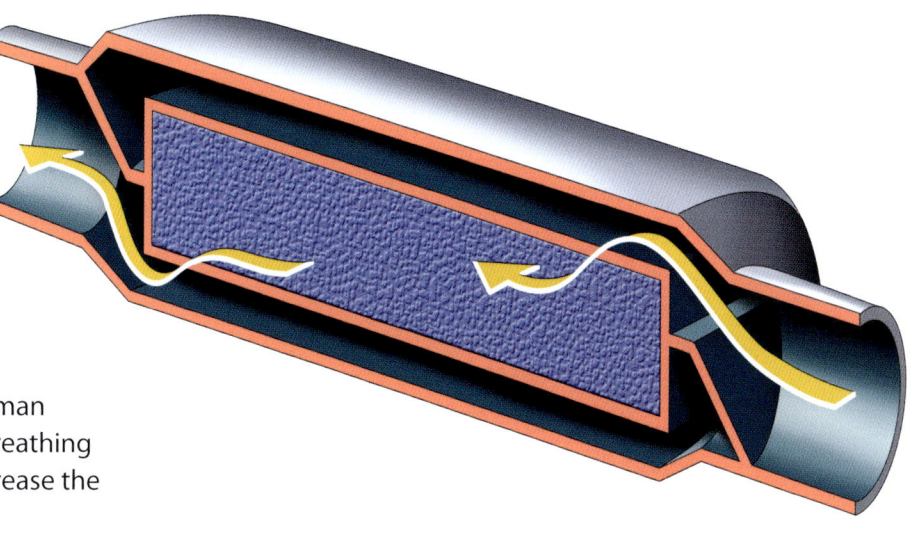

Certain measures have been taken by the UK government to try to minimise the effects of pollution. Legislation was introduced in 2001 to try to discourage motorists from driving vehicles with high exhaust emissions and to encourage the purchase of less polluting models. Every vehicle was given its own specific VED tax grouping, ranging from A–G (A the least expensive and G the most expensive) and costing from £0 to £400, depending on the amount of exhaust emissions. In April 2009 these tax groupings increased from A–M, increasing taxation on high polluting vehicles. The higher the exhaust emissions, the more expensive the vehicle excise duty. Sports cars, 4×4s, vehicles with bigger engines or twin exhausts will all have high tax groupings because of the large amounts of exhaust emissions that they emit. This legislation aims to persuade motorists to think twice about the type of vehicle they drive, reducing unnecessary exhaust emissions and therefore damage to the environment. For example, a couple with one child will generally not need a large, 4×4 jeep to leave the child to school and to do the shopping. A smaller vehicle would emit less exhaust gases into the atmosphere, would use less fuel and have a lower level of VED, therefore making it more economical to run.

The introduction of lead-free petrol has helped to reduce pollution. Engines need to run at their highest level and require good fuel to do so. Four-star petrol used to be of a slightly better quality than unleaded and therefore motorists were more likely to purchase it. In recent years, a new 'super' unleaded fuel, LRP (Lead Replacement Petrol), has replaced the more damaging, lead carrying, four-star fuel. Filling stations no longer sell four-star petrol.

Exhaust gases are not the only forms of pollution. Some motorists throw litter out of their vehicles while driving, which can injure wildlife and spoil the countryside.

Efforts to reduce pollution...

▶ As already discussed on page 68, noise pollution is a common problem, especially in towns and cities. Busy roads, railways and airports close to residential areas can annoy inhabitants. The occupants of these houses sometimes have to spend more money on sound insulation to reduce external noise.

FOR YOUR FOLDER

1. Why is air pollution from exhaust gases a very serious problem?
2. List some exhaust gases.
3. What effect does carbon monoxide have on the body?
4. What exhaust gas is a major contributor to climate change?
5. How would you describe hydrocarbons and what do they do to the body?
6. How do vehicle manufacturers help to reduce exhaust emissions?

FOR YOUR FOLDER

7. What exhaust gases do catalytic converters remove?
8. What measures have been taken to remove lead as a major pollutant?
9. What do the letters LRP stand for?
10. Apart from exhaust gases, name two other types of pollution that motorists and their vehicles can cause.

MOTORING LAWS

All pupils should be able to give a brief explanation to demonstrate their knowledge of the following motoring laws.

The Locomotives Act (The Red Flag Act) 1865

- this act required three persons to drive or conduct every locomotive propelled by steam or any other power (except animal power).
- at least one of these persons should walk at least 60 yards in front and carry a red flag to warn riders and drivers of horses.
- this act set the speed limit at 4 mph and at 2 mph through a city, town or village.

The Motor Car Act 1903
This act:
- adopted the term 'motor car'.
- introduced the requirement to register a motor car with a county or borough council.
- introduced registration (number) plates.
- introduced licensing of drivers by county or borough councils.
- set the licence fee.
- set the qualifying age for a motor car licence at 17 and the age for a motorcycle licence at 14.
- introduced suspension, disqualification and endorsement of licences.

The Road Traffic Act (Northern Ireland) 1955
This act brought legislation in Northern Ireland into line with that in Great Britain and introduced:
- provisional licences, driving tests and regulations regarding physical fitness and age qualification (17 for car drivers and 16 for motorcyclists).
- driving offences (dangerous and careless driving, driving under the influence of drink or drugs and driving while uninsured).
- disqualification from driving.
- offences by pedestrians, cyclists and motorcyclists.
- the issue of the *Highway Code*.

The Road Traffic Act 1967/Road Safety Act 1967
This act introduced the first maximum legal blood alcohol (drink driving) limit in the UK. The defined maximum Blood Alcohol Concentration (BAC) levels are:
- 35 micrograms of alcohol per 100 millilitres of breath
- 80 milligrams of alcohol per 100 millilitres of blood
- 107 milligrams of alcohol per 100 millilitres of urine

The Road Traffic (Seat Belts) (NI) Order 1981
- this order empowered the Department of Education to make regulations requiring adults to wear seat belts in the front and rear seats, and children to wear seat belts in the front seats.
- regulations relating to the front seats were introduced on 31 January 1983.
- regulations relating to adults in the rear were introduced on 1 July 1991.

The Motor Vehicles (Wearing of Rear Seat Belts by Children) (NI) Order 1989
- This order required children to wear seat belts in the rear and that the regulations became operative on 1 September 1989.

The Road Traffic (Amendment) (NI) Order 1991
- this order made fresh provision in respect of offences arising out of driving or being in charge of a motor vehicle while under the influence of drink or drugs.
- including an obligatory minimum disqualification period of 12 months and the requirement to resit the driving test, if convicted.

The Road Traffic Offenders (NI) Order 1996
This order introduced a system of penalty points, as follows:
- road traffic offences are separated into those which involve obligatory endorsement and those which are not endorsable.
- endorsable offences carry a number or range of penalty points which are endorsed on the counterpart of the licence in all situations where a court, convicting a person of an offence involving obligatory endorsement, does not order disqualification.
- where a driver accumulates 12 or more points within a three-year period, he or she is subject to a period of disqualification. This is for a period of six months, but this

MOTORING LAWS...

can be increased to one or two years, depending on the number of previous disqualifications in the preceding three years.

The Road Traffic (NI) Order 2007
This order introduced a range of measures, as follows:
- penalty points for non-wearing of seat belts and for using a hand-held mobile phone while driving.
- gave the power to courts to make use of re-training courses for drink/drive offences.
- an on-the-spot fixed penalty deposit scheme and powers to issue fixed penalties to drivers without a UK licence (to prevent foreign drivers escaping penalties).
- gave police powers to seize and dispose of vehicles if driven without insurance.
- a new system of endorsement which allowed EU drivers to avail of the fixed penalty system rather than having to appear in court.
- the vehicle test (MOT) disc to be displayed on the windscreen.
- an approved test assistant to help an applicant during the driving test if the applicant has hearing difficulties or difficulties understanding or responding to instructions, for example language translators.

Source: Appendix 2, CCEA Motor Vehicle and Road User Studies Specification (2017)

Chapter Four

MOTORING MATHEMATICS

BUYING A VEHICLE

Most teenagers passing their driving test at 17 years old would like to own their own car so that they can have more freedom and independence. Cars seem more expensive to buy whenever you are young. You may still be in full time education, with only a part-time job, or you may be an apprentice, having only started out in your chosen career. It takes a few years to gather up enough money to buy a vehicle. Some people are fortunate enough that a parent includes them on their insurance for a couple of years. Others might even have a car bought for them. But the majority of teenagers will have to save to buy their own.

Many factors influence the overall cost of owning a vehicle and there are many opportunities for borrowing money. However, you need to be careful that you can comfortably pay back any money you borrow and not get yourself into any difficulty with debt. The cost of borrowing needs to be carefully considered by looking at the positives and negatives of each method.

The term 'straight sale' simply means buying a vehicle without trading in another against it. The buying of brand new vehicle is normally a straight sale. New vehicles are usually bought with warranties, which cover them for a set period of time, usually years, against mechanical faults. If your vehicle is deemed to have a serious mechanical fault while under warranty most manufacturers will replace it if the fault cannot be sorted out by the specialist manufacturer. Unfortunately, a second-hand vehicle (especially if it is older than two or three years) will not usually be covered by warranty and you can never be sure how reliable the vehicle will be.

When purchasing a vehicle you should always ask to see the V5 form to see how many previous owners the vehicle has had. A vehicle with numerous owners may be an indicator of a troublesome vehicle. You should also enquire about, and look to see, the vehicle's full service history and should ask if the vehicle has a valid MOT certificate, as this document indicates

roadworthiness. Some vehicle owners will trade their old vehicle in against a new one to help reduce costs. Other people would rather buy privately than go to a car dealer. Dealers are always looking to get their percentage profit out of the vehicle; therefore it can be cheaper to buy privately. A dealer's reputation is in the back of most people's minds when looking for a second-hand vehicle, as information such as mileage can be misleading if tampered with. It is very important that you give a second-hand vehicle a thorough examination before purchasing it. It is also always wise to seek a second opinion, even from your mechanic, before committing yourself to buy.

If you can afford it, a brand new vehicle has a few advantages. The vehicle should be in perfect, roadworthy condition when purchased and therefore will not legally require an MOT test for its first four years. If driven and maintained with care it should not need very many repairs in that time and should have lower running costs than an older car. The main disadvantage of buying a new car is the cost, which will be much more than that of a second-hand purchase. However, banks and credit companies will often allow monthly repayments to make purchasing a new vehicle more manageable.

FOR YOUR FOLDER

1. What is meant by the term 'straight sale'?
2. What is meant by the term 'vehicle under warranty'?
3. What two documents should you ask to see when purchasing a second-hand vehicle?
4. Why would some vehicle owners trade in their old vehicle against a newer model?
5. Why are some people cautious of buying an older, second-hand vehicle from a car dealer?

MOTORING COSTS

There are four main costs associated with owning a vehicle:

1. **Purchasing costs** – how much and what method is used to pay for the vehicle.
2. **Standing costs** – what legal documents are required before a driver or vehicle can use the roads.
3. **Running costs** – how much it costs to keep a vehicle on the road.
4. **Additional costs** – hidden costs that many motorists forget about.

Purchasing costs

When buying a vehicle you can pay for it using ready cash that you have saved up over a period of time. This is the cheapest option for buying a vehicle but it does take time to save the money. Not everyone is in a position to pay cash for a vehicle and may therefore need to borrow money.

There are many different banks, credit facilities and finance companies all willing to lend money but at a cost. This cost will depend on the monthly rate of interest being charged on the amount borrowed. If you borrow money for buying a vehicle you will have to pay interest back on the loan, which will increase the overall cost. This interest is usually known as 'APR' (Annual Percentage Rate). The APR will tell you how expensive the loan will be and how much interest will be charged each year. These repayments will be made monthly. Loans taken out on 'HP' (Hire Purchase) from HP companies often have a higher APR than loans from banks. It is

Standing costs

These costs are legal requirements and need documentation to prove that a vehicle is legally entitled to use the roads.

- Insurance is usually the most expensive of these costs and is renewed each year. A certificate of insurance is the legal document needed.
- Any vehicle driver using the roads must pass the official driving test. A driving licence is the official document that proves that a driver has passed this test. The cost to sit the theory test in Northern Ireland, in 2024, was £23 and the practical driving test was £65. Both parts must be passed to obtain a driver's licence. The cost of driving lessons (in 2024) was approximately £28–£32.
- Vehicle Excise Duty (VED, sometimes referred to incorrectly as 'road tax') is another legal requirement and has to be renewed every year.

important, therefore, that you shop around for the best loan deal, as APR rates will vary. Bank loans are usually the cheapest form of borrowing because interest rates vary and are only charged on the opening balance of the loan. Loans borrowed from finance companies will require you to pay a percentage cost for a vehicle up front and the interest will then be charged on the remaining amount. For example, if you had to pay 20% of a vehicle costing £10,000, you would have to pay £2000 up front and then pay a monthly interest rate on the remaining £8000. Using credit facilities enables you to pay for your vehicle monthly over a period of years. This may take the financial pressure off you at the time of buying the vehicle but in the long term the overall cost of the vehicle will work out more than the original price. Some cars dealers offer deals to newly qualified drivers, such as free insurance for a set period of years, to encourage them to buy a brand new vehicle.

Some people may wish to lease a vehicle, which means that they are renting a vehicle for a number of years. What they are really paying for is the amount that the vehicle de-values during each year of the lease. Some people may make a down payment at the start of a lease to reduce the size of their monthly payments. The two main advantages of leasing are the lower monthly payments and the opportunity to have a new vehicle every few years.

- Vehicles over four years of age must pass an annual MOT inspection. On passing the test, an MOT examiner will issue an MOT certificate as proof that the vehicle was roadworthy at the time of the test. The cost to MOT a vehicle in 2024 was £38 but this does not include the cost of preparing the vehicle. It is wise to have a mechanic service or check over your vehicle and carry out the necessary repairs to ensure the vehicle has the best possible chance of passing the test. Depending on how well the vehicle is looked after, these mechanical costs vary, but they can be quite expensive.
- Many motorists also forget the hidden cost of depreciation. This is the amount that the value of your vehicle decreases each year that you own it.

Running costs

These are the everyday costs that are needed to run a vehicle. The most expensive of these costs is purchasing fuel. Some vehicles are more economical with fuel than others. Factors that can influence fuel usage are the size of the engine, acceleration, speed, and distance of journey. Another running cost is the cost of getting your car serviced and this is advised every 10,000 miles to ensure the best performance from your vehicle. Vehicles regularly need servicing to ensure the full safety of its occupants. Such repairs or replacements might include oil, air or fuel filters; tyres; lights; brake pads; clutch cables; and exhausts. Tyres and replacement bulbs are some of the more regular replacements needed. Owning a troublesome vehicle can be very costly, so it is very important to look after your vehicle to ensure that it runs as smoothly as possible. Servicing in a garage can be quite expensive. Not only do the parts have to be paid for but the mechanic's time (labour) must be paid for also. For this reason many people, with sufficient knowledge and ability, carry out what DIY repairs they can do themselves to try to reduce the overall cost of servicing.

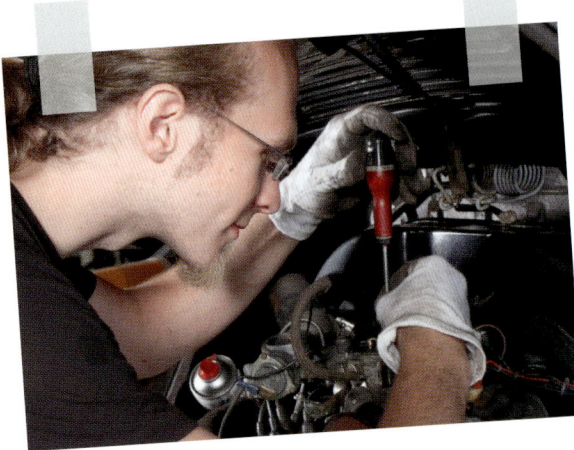

To make running cost payments more manageable some people will set up monthly accounts, for example with fuel companies, so that they can fill their vehicle when needed without having to pay immediately. A monthly statement would then be sent out requesting payment and showing the number of litres purchased. Alternatively, direct debits can be set up. This allows payments to be taken out of an account on an agreed date each month. Credit cards can also be used to make payments but these generally accrue a lot of interest if the balance is not paid off every month. Some businesses may offer inducements on fuel or parts. Inducements are incentives, usually a reduced price, used to encourage customers to purchase another product or service from the same company.

Additional costs

There are a few other costs that may add to the expense of owning a vehicle, such as parking fees and garaging. Some motorists may even pick up fines for parking and speeding, which can add to the cost of motoring. If you decide to take money from an investment (savings) to buy your car, you will lose the interest you would have earned on that investment, as well as the depreciation in the value of the car. This is known as interest on capital investment.

Clothing and footwear, especially for cyclists and motorcyclists, can be quite expensive. Leather and padded clothes to protect the rider can also be pricey, as can the essential safety items, such as helmets and reflective gear. The cost of cleaning and lubricating materials and liquids also needs budgeted for. Similarly, if you plan to add a lot of extras to your car, remember media players, alloy wheels, spoilers and exhausts will all add up!

7. Start the vehicle, take it for a test drive and try all the gears and electrics.
8. Check under the bonnet for a clean engine, clear of oil and leaks. Also check under the vehicle for signs of rust, wear and tear, and leaks.
9. Check that all seat belts fasten and that the inside of the vehicle is in a clean and healthy condition.
10. Ask plenty of questions about the vehicle and always try to negotiate a cheaper price.

How to buy a second-hand vehicle

1. Never rush into a purchase. Always check local papers, Internet websites and car dealers to see if a vehicle is similarly and reasonably priced elsewhere.
2. Try to take someone experienced with you. A second opinion is priceless.
3. Always view a vehicle in daylight.
4. Check the V5 form for the number of previous owners and check if the vehicle has an MOT certificate.
5. Check the mileage and ask about the vehicle's service history. The service book should show the mileage at the last service and should have a record of all repairs. The MOT certificate should also show the mileage. Check the condition of the tyres.
6. Carry out a thorough inspection of the bodywork for rust and dents.

FOR YOUR FOLDER

1. What are the two most common methods of purchasing a vehicle?
2. What does HP stand for?
3. Briefly explain how buying a vehicle through a finance company works.
4. Name four standing costs that must be covered by a vehicle owner.
5. What is meant by the term depreciation?

FOR YOUR FOLDER

6. What are running costs?
7. Make a list of the typical running costs of a vehicle.
8. How often is it recommended that you get your vehicle serviced?
9. List four additional costs that can add to the expense of owning a vehicle.
10. List four main points to remember when buying a second-hand vehicle.

CALCULATING COSTS

In order to keep your motoring costs as low as possible there are a number of ways that you can adapt your driving to save fuel. Fuel consumption is the most expensive running cost and a number of steps can be taken to reduce it. You should:

- Avoid unnecessary and short trips in your vehicle.
- Drive with care, avoid sudden acceleration and sharp braking. Sharp braking will increase tyre wear, reducing grip and increasing braking distances.
- Use air conditioning only when it is absolutely necessary as it increases fuel consumption by about 10%.
- Ensure your tyres are at the correct pressure so that your vehicle is easy to steer and handle. Good tyres improve a vehicle's performance and help reduce fuel consumption.
- Use higher gears and keep to speed limits to save fuel.

These tips will also help a vehicle to perform better on the roads, save fuel through careful driving and increase the MPG (miles per gallon). MPG is a measure of how many miles a vehicle can travel on one gallon of fuel. To calculate the average speed for a journey the total distance is divided by the total time. Keeping at the same average speed over a journey saves fuel and therefore helps to reduce running costs. Some vehicles perform better than others and will therefore travel a greater distance than others on one gallon of fuel. It is a good idea to ask about the fuel consumption of a vehicle before purchasing it, as you may be considering buying a vehicle that uses a lot of fuel. Statistics have shown that if all vehicles were driven at half the average speed we would save 75% on fuel consumption. Therefore if we drive our vehicles carefully and at the correct speed, we could save a lot of fuel.

Careful drivers will ultimately reduce maintenance costs by avoiding harsh braking and steering. Speeding drivers will use more fuel and increase braking and stopping distances. These increases will accelerate tyre wear and reduce the effectiveness of the brake pads, parts of the steering and the suspension system. More regular garage visits and maintenance repairs will probably be needed as a result, increasing their vehicle's running costs.

Travel graphs are used to calculate time, distance, speed and to illustrate a road user's journey. They can also be used to calculate average speeds for different sections of a route and to illustrate more than one journey on each graph. The example graph opposite gives information on the distance of a cyclist from his home and is a type of question that can be asked on a GCSE paper.

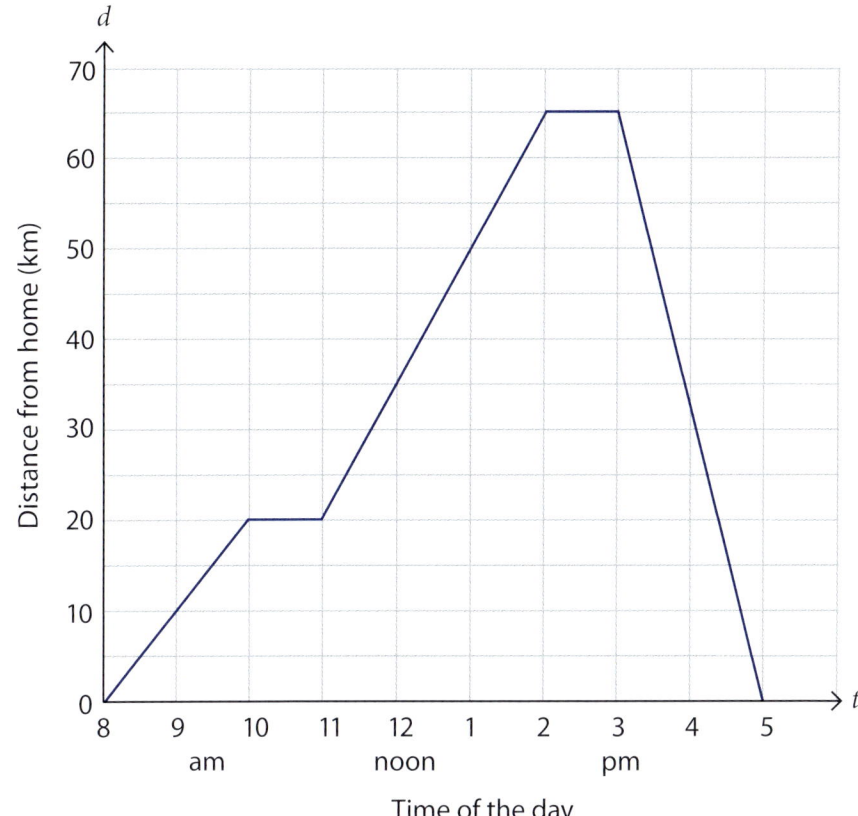

Use the questions below to test how well you understand this graph. The answers are given at the bottom of the page.

1. When did the cyclist leave home?
2. When did the cyclist return home?
3. How far from home was he at 11 am?
4. How far from home was he at 2 pm?
5. How far from home was he at 3 pm?
6. How far from home was he at 5 pm?
7. At what times did he stop for a rest?
8. Work out his speed from:
   (a) 8 am to 9 pm
   (b) 12 pm to 2 pm
   (c) 3 pm to 5 pm
9. Between what times was the cyclist travelling most quickly?

A Hyundai iX35 is priced in the auto trader magazine at £5799. Purchasers must also pay an indemnity fee of £51, a number plate surcharge of £40 and twelve months' VED of £110.

(a) What is the total cost of the vehicle?

(b) Calculate the cost per month over 36 months, if there is a 20% deposit and interest is charged at 15% per annum (assume that all interest is calculated at the start).

(a)
Cost of vehicle = 5799 + 51 + 40 + 110 = **£6000**

(b)
Deposit = 20% of cost of vehicle = $\dfrac{6000 \times 20}{100}$ = £1200

Interest will be charged on cost of vehicle − deposit
= 6000 − 1200
= £4800

Interest per annum (per year)
= 15% of cost that the interest will be charged on
= $\dfrac{4800 \times 15}{100}$ = £720

Answers: (1) 8 am (2) 5 pm (3) 20 km (4) 65 km (5) 65 km (6) 0 km (7) 10–11 am and 2–3 pm (8)(a) 10 km/h (b) 15 km/h (c) 32.5 km/h (9) 3–5 pm

Examples...

Key word...
An **indemnity fee** is paid on top of the purchase price so that legal checks can be carried out on the vehicle to ensure, for example, that the chassis number is correct or that the vehicle has not been stolen.

continued...

Total interest charged over 36 months
= interest per annum × 3 years
= £720 × 3
= £2160

Total cost of vehicle with interest (not including deposit)
= £4800 + £2160
= £6960

Therefore, cost per month
= total cost of vehicle (including interest) ÷ 36 months
= £6960 ÷ 36
= £193.33

2

A car costs £15 500. If I pay cash I will receive a discount of 10% plus cash back of £1000.

How much extra will I pay if I use vehicle finance, on the full purchase price, with a 20% deposit and 36 monthly payments of £395 per month?

Discount = 10% of £15 500
$= \dfrac{15\,500 \times 10}{100} = £1550$

Cash cost = car cost − discount − cash back
= £15 500 − £1550 − £1000
= £12 950

Deposit = 20% of car cost
$= \dfrac{15\,500 \times 20}{100} = £3100$

Total cost of monthly repayments
= 36 monthly payments at £395
= 36 × £395
= £14 220

Finance cost
= deposit + 36 monthly payments
= £3100 + £14 220
= £17 320

Extra paid with vehicle finance
= finance cost − cash cost
= £17 320 − £12 950
= **£4370**

3

A brand new car costs £22 145.

(a) Calculate its value after one year if it loses 20% in the first 12 months.

(b) Calculate the percentage depreciation over 3 years, if its value drops to £13 287 over that period.

(a)

Loss in first 12 months = 20% of cost

$$= \frac{£22\,145 \times 20}{100} = £4429$$

Value after one year
= cost − loss in first year
= £22 145 − £4429
= **£17 716**

(b)

Dropped value = $\dfrac{\text{value after 3 years}}{\text{original price}} \times 100$

$= \dfrac{13\,287}{22\,145} \times 100 = 60\%$

If the original price = 100%
then the dropped price = 60%

Percentage depreciation
= 100% − 60%
= **40%**

FOR YOUR FOLDER

1. A new Audi sports car costs £27 000. You have asked for a personalised number plate costing £75 and a set of Audi alloy wheels costing £450 to be fitted. You will leave a deposit of £5000 and use vehicle finance to pay the remaining sum over 5 years.
    (a) Calculate the total cost of the vehicle.
    (b) Calculate the cost of the monthly payments over 5 years.

2. A Renault Zoe is priced in an auto trader magazine at £7000. Purchasers must also pay an indemnity fee of £67 and twelve months' VED of £185.
    (a) What is the total cost of the vehicle?
    (b) Calculate the cost per month, over 60 months, if there is a 30% deposit and interest is charged at 17.5%.

FOR YOUR FOLDER

3. A driver travels at an average speed of 56 mph for 3 hours.
    (a) How far has the vehicle travelled?
    (b) A motorist travels at an average speed of 50 mph for 2 hours and spends 3 hours travelling the remaining 60 miles.
        (i) What is the total distance travelled?
        (ii) What is the average speed for the whole journey?

4. In the cooling system of a car engine, anti-freeze and water have to be mixed at a ratio of 1:4. If 0.5 litres of anti-freeze is to be used, how much water must be added?

Chapter Five

COLLISION PROCEDURES

INVOLVEMENT IN A COLLISION

Road traffic collisions can take many shapes and forms. In all cases the driver must stop at the scene to report the collision. Collisions may involve:

- **Vehicles**
- **Pedestrians**
- **Cyclists**
- **Animals**
- **Property, signs or trees**

If involved in a serious collision, all personnel involved must remain at the scene and the police should be contacted. All occupants have a legal obligation to give their personal details to the police. In some instances motorists may not send for the police and may sort damages out between themselves. This will happen only if the party at fault accepts responsibility, no occupants are injured, all parties are agreed and the cost to repair damages is deemed to be affordable. Motorists may wish to do this to avoid involving their insurance companies, which could result in a higher insurance premium the next year and a loss of their no claims bonus. However, the collision must still be reported to the police within twenty-four hours. The information that needs to be shared and exchanged at the scene of a collision is shown in the box.

- The name and addresses of all parties involved.
- The personal details of the vehicle owner.
- The vehicle registration number.

This information should be given at the collision scene and if not exchanged then it must be reported to the police within twenty-four hours. Motorists will also be asked to produce their insurance documentation and the driver could be charged with 'hit and run' if they leave the scene or delay notifying the police unnecessarily.

Insurance companies will advise you never to accept responsibility for a collision. If you do not admit that the collision was your fault they may be able to legally defend your driving. If they successfully prove that the collision was not your fault they will not have to pay for the damages caused to the other parties involved. Insurance companies cannot proceed with a claim if the collision has not been reported to the police. In some instances the police may not come out to the scene. However, they will always visit the scene if someone has been injured or if the vehicles are badly damaged, cannot be moved or are causing a road obstruction. If the police do not come out and you think that insurance companies may have to be involved, it is wise to take a photograph of the scene, especially if you are not at fault.

POST-COLLISION PROCEDURE

Most people do not know what to do upon witnessing a collision, other than looking on horrified and shocked. However, the minutes following a collision are often critical as an injured person's chances of survival may be at risk. A person who knows exactly what to do may give first aid treatment and possibly save a life. This person should be able to address the following five main priorities in a calm and constructive manner.

Secure the scene of the collision

This involves **warning other road users** that a collision has happened. Use your hazard warning lights and if possible place a warning triangle at least 45 metres in front of the scene. You should also remember to **protect yourself**, ensuring you are easy to see. This can be achieved by wearing fluorescent or bright materials and by carrying a torch to wave down approaching traffic.

Summon help from the emergency services – dial 999

Emergency services:
- Police
- Ambulance
- Fire Brigade

Tell them:
- The location of the collision.
- The number of injured victims.
- If there is anyone trapped.
- Whether there is any risk of fire.
- How many vehicles are involved (if any).

On motorways emergency phones can be found by following arrows marked alongside the carriageway. They will put you directly through to the police.

Check that vehicles are safe to approach

Be aware of fuel leaks as any spark could cause an explosion.

Check that vehicles are safe

Two tasks should be carried out:
- Switch off the ignition.
- Put the handbrake on.

If it is not possible to put the handbrake on, the wheels should be choked with stones or wood to prevent the vehicle from moving, especially on a hill. You should also insist that nobody smokes. If a fire breaks out, try to tackle it with a fire extinguisher or smother it with a blanket. If it gets out of hand, only then should you try to remove injured people from the vehicle.

Investigate casualties

Always check individuals in a vehicle who are quiet to begin with. The first aid priorities are:

Make sure the person is conscious: A person may be unconscious if they are unresponsive to your voice or gentle shaking. However, do not shake a casualty if they may have a neck or back injury.

Make sure the person is breathing properly: Check the casualty's breathing and ensure that blood, vomit or the tongue are not blocking the air passage. If the casualty is not breathing commence emergency resuscitation to keep the heart pumping blood around the body, especially to the brain. If the brain is deprived of oxygen for more than four minutes, permanent damage could occur. The most effective method of resuscitation is mouth-to-mouth, which is performed by completing the following steps:

1. Take a deep breath, pulling air back into your lungs.
2. Pinch the casualty's nostrils with your fingers.
3. Seal your lips around the casualty's mouth.
4. Blow into the casualty's lungs until the chest rises.
5. Remove your mouth and watch for the chest falling.
6. Repeat this process until the casualty begins to breath again unassisted or the emergency services arrive.

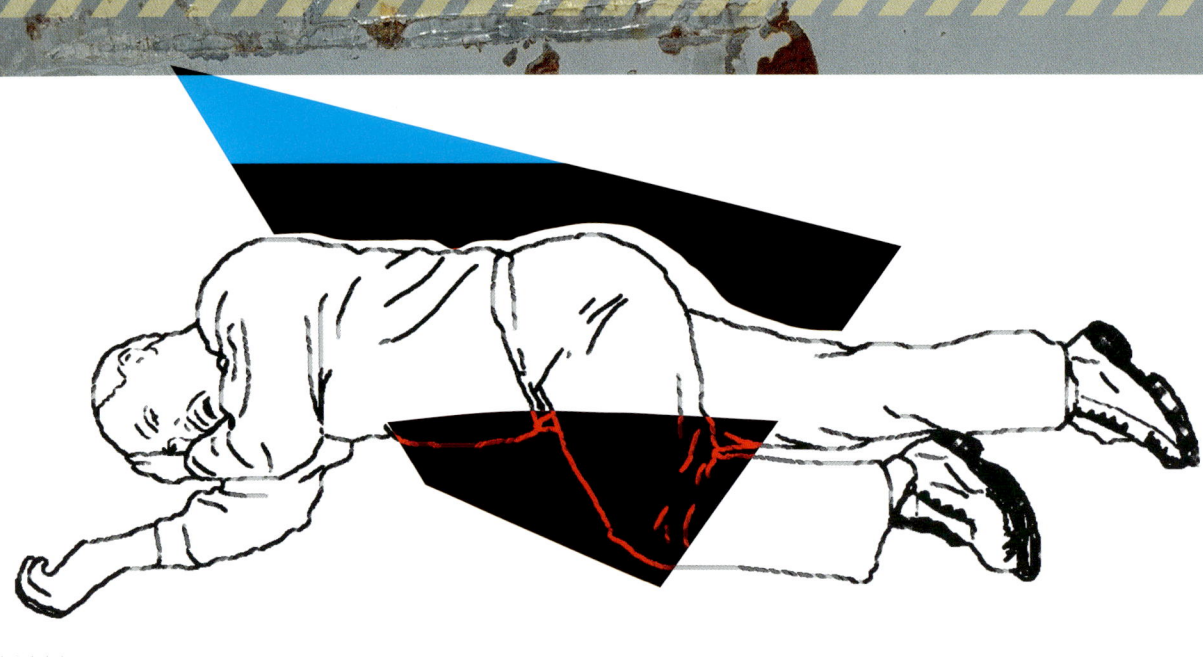

If the casualty is breathing but lying forward, push the person back to sit upright, which should improve his or her breathing. If breathing but unconscious it may be necessary to place the casualty in the recovery position. The recovery position is used to tilt the mouth downwards to allow any fluids to drain out of the mouth and to prevent a casualty from swallowing his or her tongue. This is very important because if the fluids were allowed to flow back down the throat a person could choke, drown or suffocate. To place someone in the recovery position turn the person onto his or her side, lift the chin forward so that the airway is open and place the hand underneath the cheek to prevent rolling.

Check the casualty in case they are suffering from shock: The symptoms of shock include the following:

- The casualty looks pale, feels faint or dizzy.
- The casualty's breathing has become shallow but quick.
- The casualty's pulse is weak but quick.
- The casualty feels sick or vomits.
- The casualty is thirsty.

If you assume a person is in shock you should immediately sit the person down, with the head kept low and turned to one side. If possible the lower limbs should be slightly raised. Loosen the casualty's clothing, especially around the neck, chest and waist, and wrap extra clothing or blankets around the body to maintain heat. Do not give the person anything to eat or drink in case they have injured themselves and need medical attention requiring an anaesthetic. Keep checking that the casualty is breathing and offer plenty of reassurance.

Stop or reduce bleeding: Apply pressure to the wound, avoiding any foreign bodies. Use a clean cloth, handkerchief or paper tissues to cover the wound. There are a number of different types of wounds and it is important that we understand how to treat them:

Stop or reduce bleeding...

- **Incised wounds** – These are open, cut-like injuries made by a sharp object such as broken glass. If the wound is bleeding heavily it should be covered with a cloth and pressure applied to stop the bleeding.
- **Lacerated wounds** – These are caused by impact, usually due to being thrown about inside a vehicle. The result is a crushing of bones, and a ripping and tearing of flesh.
- **Contused wounds** – These are injuries caused without breaking the skin. They are closed wounds, for example bruising, and are usually inflicted by a blunt instrument.
- **Punctured wounds** – These are open wounds caused by something striking the individual and piercing the skin. Common injuries are punctured lungs and kidneys. In some severe cases the object causing the puncture may get stuck inside the victim and remain there until removed in an operating theatre.

ABC...

First aid procedures

Remember, always follow the ABC of First Aid:

A is for Airway: A blocked airway can restrict a casualty's ability to breathe. To open a casualty's airway follow these steps:

1. Put one hand on the casualty's forehead.
2. Gently tilt the head back.
3. When tilting the head, use the other hand to carefully raise their chin.

B is for Breathing: Check if the person is still breathing. Breathing supplies the body with life-giving oxygen.

1. Put your ear directly above the casualty's mouth and nose listening for breathing sounds.
2. Look to see if their chest is rising and falling.
3. Check for the feel of their breath against your cheek for ten seconds. If they are breathing normally, the casualty should be placed in the recovery position.

C is for Circulation: If the casualty isn't breathing, immediately start chest compressions to restore blood circulation in the body. Dial 999 and request an ambulance.

PRECAUTIONS

A realistic road user will always be prepared for the unexpected, as their vehicle may break down or be involved in a collision at any time during their driving career. It is important to be prepared and carry the following items:

- A complete set of replacement bulbs.
- A notebook and pen.
- A torch.
- A fire extinguisher.
- A warning triangle.
- Reflective/fluorescent bands or jacket.
- A first aid kit containing bandages.
- A mobile phone.

FOR YOUR FOLDER

1. What is the first thing a passer-by should do at the scene of a collision?
2. List, in order, the five main steps that should be followed at the scene of a collision.
3. What information should be given to the emergency services?
4. How would you contact the emergency services?
5. Make a list of items that would be useful at the scene of a collision.
6. What is a contused wound?
7. What is a lacerated wound?
8. What is the ABC of First Aid?

Chapter Six
MOTOR VEHICLE TECHNOLOGY

When designing and manufacturing vehicles, different manufacturing companies have their own unique shapes and designs. However, they all must make sure that their vehicles keep the occupants safe, comfortable and perform safely on the roads. The frame or design of a vehicle consists of two main parts, within which the remainder of the systems are built or connected: **the vehicle body** and **the vehicle chassis.**

The body can be defined as the skeleton or shell that holds all the vehicle systems together. It must be built to protect from natural elements, such as adverse weather conditions, and also to protect its occupants in the event of an accident. For example, vehicle doors have side impact bars built into them so that they will not buckle if hit with considerable force. The chassis is a strong steel frame located beneath the floor of the vehicle. Its function is to support the vehicle's bodywork and engine.

UNDERSTANDING THE CAR

Note: This section discusses the systems of a car with an internal combustion engine. Electric cars share some, but not all, of these systems.

The car is split up into a number of different parts or systems. This first diagram shows the following main parts:

- **Engine**
- **Cooling system**
- **Exhaust system**

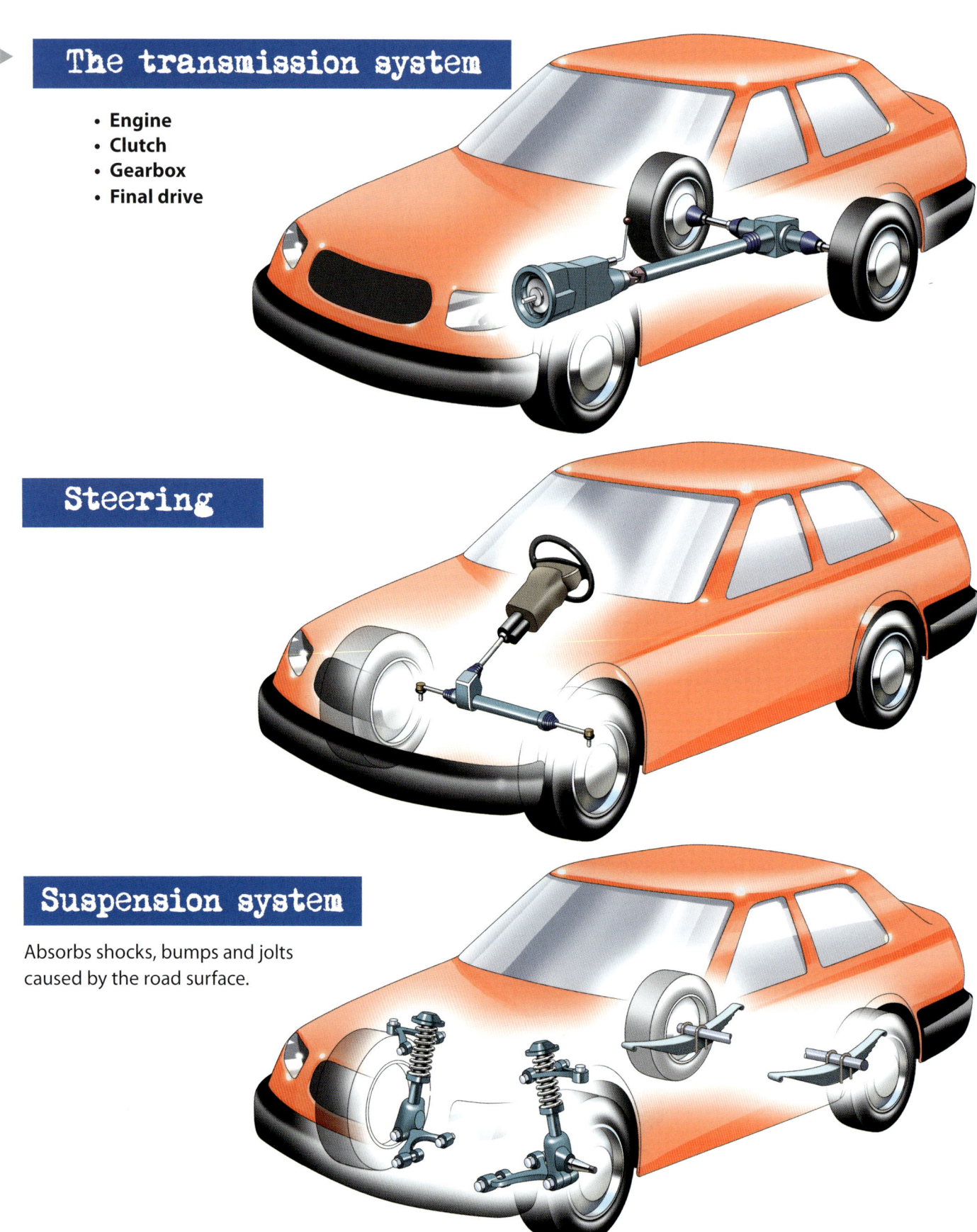

The transmission system

- **Engine**
- **Clutch**
- **Gearbox**
- **Final drive**

Steering

Suspension system

Absorbs shocks, bumps and jolts caused by the road surface.

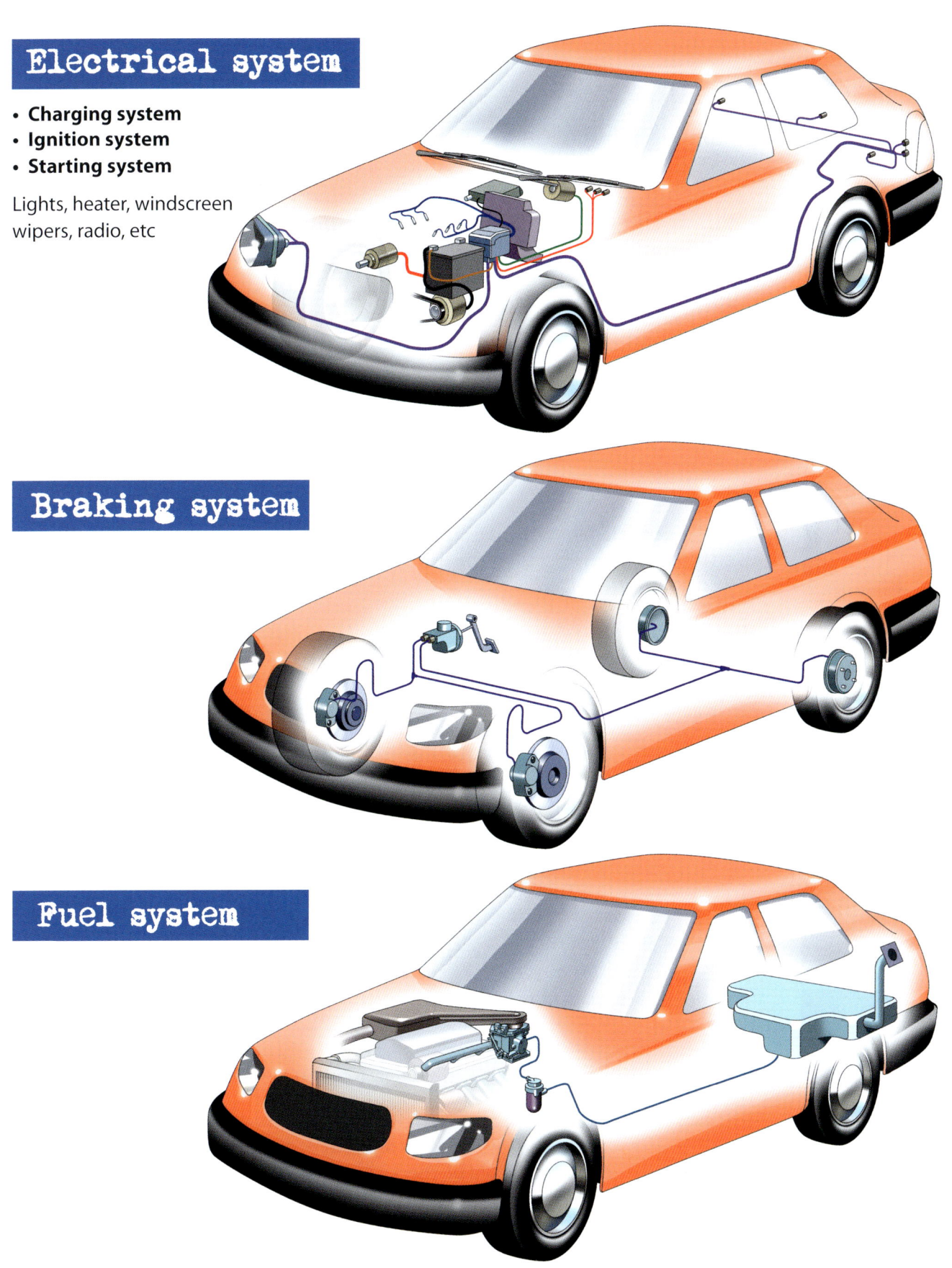

Electrical system

- **Charging system**
- **Ignition system**
- **Starting system**

Lights, heater, windscreen wipers, radio, etc

Braking system

Fuel system

ENGINE MANAGEMENT SYSTEMS

Engine management systems are built into most modern vehicles to detect any faults that may occur within the various operating systems. You will usually be made aware of a fault by a symbol lighting up on the dashboard of your vehicle. This will not tell you exactly where the fault is but you will now know to take your vehicle to a mechanic to get it checked over. The advantage of having an engine management system is that mechanics can connect the vehicle to a computerised machine in their garages to quickly detect the exact whereabouts and nature of the fault.

Some common symbols that may appear on your dashboard are:

The **engine management** light will appear on the dashboard when there is an issue with the vehicle's engine or exhaust system.

The **anti-lock brake system** light will come on if the system detects a problem with the brakes. Problems such as insufficient brake fluid in the reservoir, or a loss of traction with the road may cause the light to either come on permanently or flash momentarily on the dashboard.

The **oil** light will come on if it detects that the vehicle's oil pressure is too low. Topping the engine up with oil should result in the dashboard symbol disappearing. If it remains on there may be an oil leak, which will require a mechanic to investigate.

The **traction control** light will appear if the tyres lose contact or grip with the road. Excess speed, harsh cornering or slippery road conditions may cause this light to appear.

The **diesel particulate filter** (DPF) light is part of the exhaust system. The warning light is designed to alert the driver when the DPF filter becomes too clogged with soot and is unable to self-clean. This problem often occurs when a vehicle is regularly driven only for short distances.

The **tyre pressure** light will appear on the dashboard of a vehicle if one or more of the tyres falls below the required pressure, or if the vehicle has a puncture. The air pressure should be checked immediately to rebalance the tyres and avoid driving unsafely.

THE ELECTRICAL SYSTEM

Many motorists understand very little about how their vehicles work. Some think only about the mechanical aspects of the car and others resign themselves to knowing absolutely nothing. The car's electrical aspect can therefore be overlooked. However, a large proportion of the vehicle depends on electricity. In this section we will consider the electrical system in more detail. The electrical system is split up into three main areas:

- **The charging system**
- **The ignition system**
- **The starting system**

The alternator

Whenever an engine is started and runs for a while it uses a lot of electrical energy that was stored in the battery. The loss of this energy must be replaced otherwise the battery will drain out, the vehicle's electrics will fail and the vehicle will eventually grind to a halt. The main function of the alternator is to continually recharge the battery so that the vehicle will always start and all the electrical components will work when switched on. The alternator is driven by the fan belt, which must be put on carefully and properly tensioned. Too tight and the belt may snap. Too loose and the alternator will not charge the battery properly. A vehicle with a loose fan bet can sometimes be identified by the loud squealing noise it produces.

THE CHARGING SYSTEM

The charging system has two main components:

- **The battery**
- **The alternator**

The battery

The battery, which is usually 12 volts, provides the main source of electricity needed to power all lighting components, heaters, windscreen wipers and the radio. A battery will usually come with a two to three year guarantee but occasionally its cells may lose the ability to store electrical energy during this period. A faulty battery can lead to a vehicle becoming difficult to start. Batteries can be recharged from a mains supply; however, if it is not working properly, or continually needs to be recharged, it will never stay in a good 'live condition'.

A battery has two terminals: a positive and a negative. It stores a liquid called electrolyte, which is a mixture of water and acid, that helps to keep the battery in a lively, active condition. Be careful when connecting battery terminals, as connecting them the wrong way round could create a spark and damage the battery. Do not connect a positive lead to a negative rail. Also take care when lifting or changing a battery because acid could spill onto your clothes or skin, burning you.

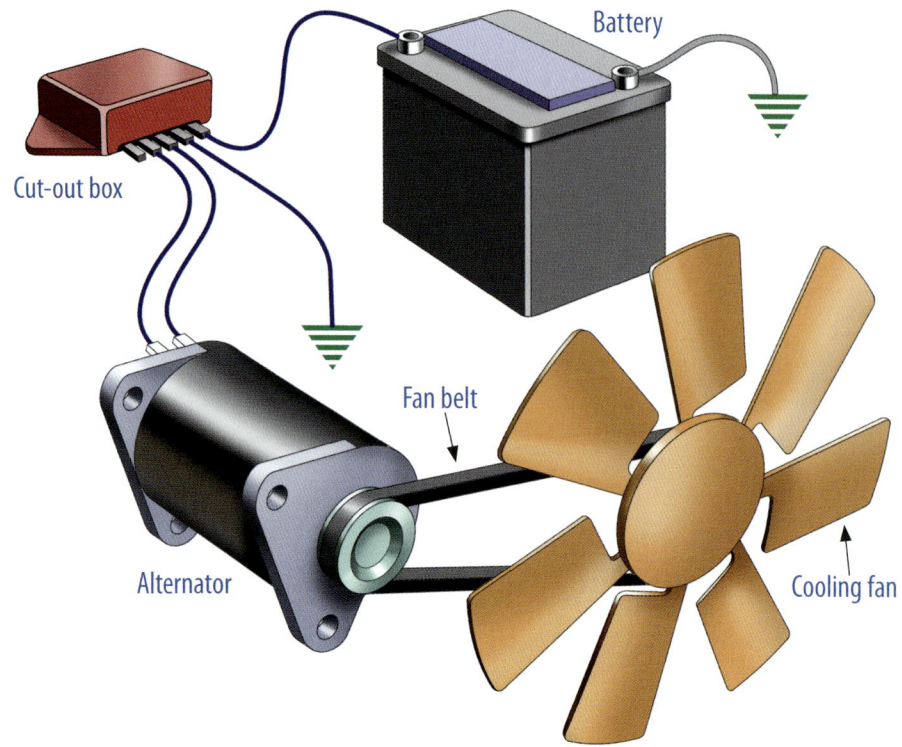

The cut-out box

A car battery needs only 12 volts to operate. Sometimes, however, the alternator can send too much current back to the battery, which can damage it. The cut-out box acts as a switch and it sometimes needs to switch off automatically to prevent the battery from being over-charged.

FOR YOUR FOLDER

1. What are the two main components of the charging system?
2. What is the main function of a battery in a car?
3. What is the name of the component that keeps the battery fully charged?
4. How does this component keep the battery fully charged?
5. What is a cut-out box? Briefly explain how it works.

THE IGNITION SYSTEM

The ignition system has a number of main components:

- **Ignition switch**
- **Coil**
- **High tension leads**
- **Distributor**
- **Spark plugs**

The ignition switch is where you insert the key to start your vehicle. On turning the key, power is allowed to travel from the battery to the coil. 12 volts from the battery is enough to turn on all the electrical components but it is not enough to start up a vehicle from cold. The function of the coil is to take the 12 volts and boost the voltage to around 30,000 volts, ensuring that enough power is generated to activate the starter motor and to create a spark in each of the spark plugs. This current is then transferred from the coil to the starter motor and spark plugs via high tension leads. The function of the spark plug is simply to create a spark like that of a cigarette lighter. Each spark plug is ignited in turn by the distributor.

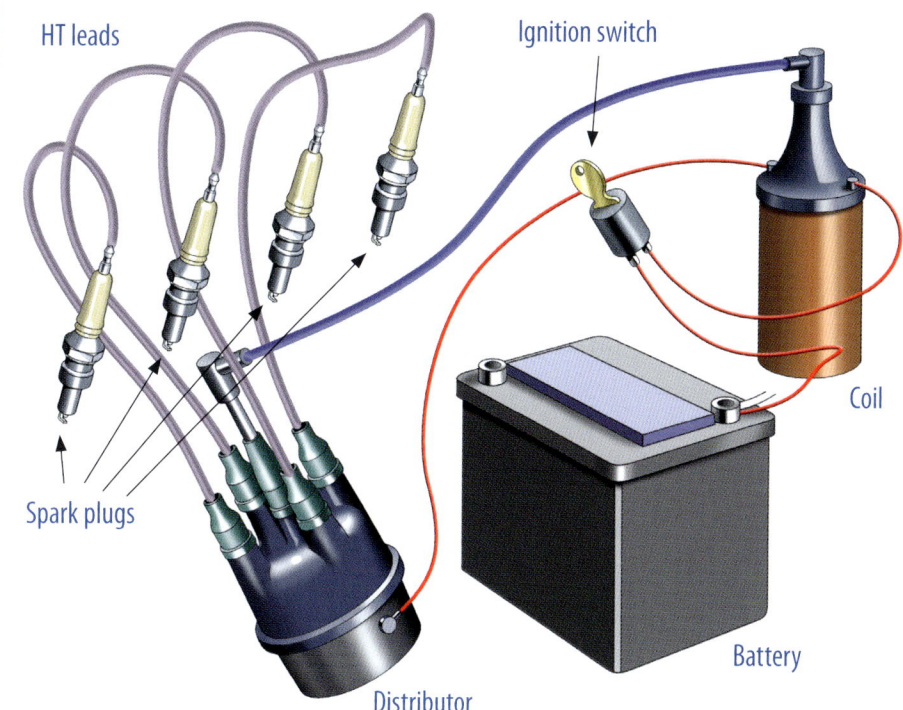

The spark plug

The main function of the spark plug is to create a spark to ignite the fuel in a vehicle's engine. **You must learn the parts of the spark plug.**

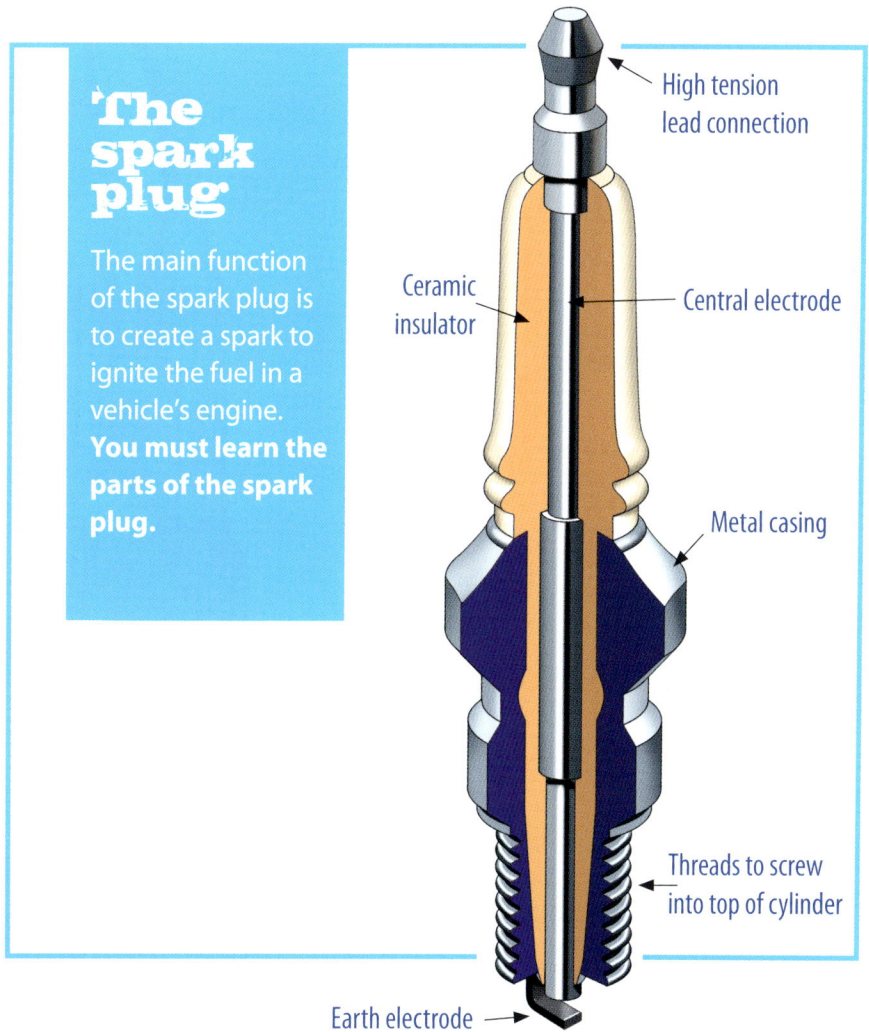

THE DISTRIBUTOR

Current is passed from the distributor to each of the four spark plugs by high tension leads. These leads are capable of carrying the high voltage current that was increased by the coil. This high voltage current is used to create a spark to ignite and burn the fuel on the power stroke of the four-stroke cycle. The rotor arm under the distributor cap rotates to strike and make an electrical connection with each of the four spark plug contacts in the required sequence.

A number of checks can be carried out c on a vehicle's electrical system by the owner:

- How secure the battery is.
- The battery connections.
- The level of electrolyte in the battery.
- The condition of plugs and wires.
- All electrical components – lights, horns, windscreen wipers, etc.

FOR YOUR FOLDER

1. What is the function of the ignition system?
2. Name the main parts of the ignition system.
3. Briefly explain how the ignition system works.
4. What is the function of the coil?
5. What is the function of a spark plug?
6. What is the distributor and how does it work?
7. What is the function of the rotor arm?
8. Make a list of the checks that can be carried out on a vehicle's electrical system.

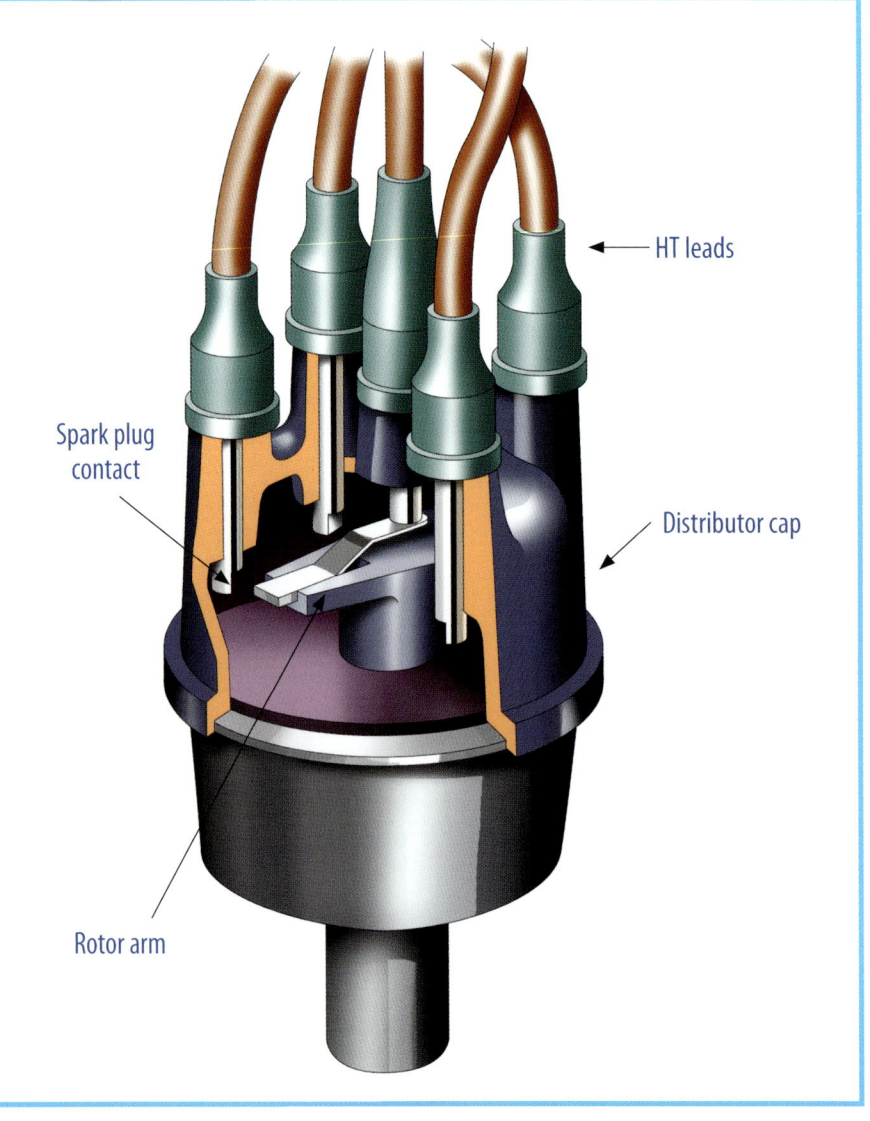

THE STARTING SYSTEM

The starting system has two main components:

- **The starter motor**
- **The solenoid**

The starter motor is the main component used to start all the moving components within the engine. It does this by turning a large, toothed flywheel, which is bolted to the crankshaft. The flywheel is toothed to engage with the starter motor and provides an even, smooth turning motion that reduces the jerky movements of the moving metal components within the engine, minimising wear and tear. Whenever the ignition switch is turned on the solenoid allows electrical power to travel to all the electrical components, such as lights and heaters. A further turn of the key against a spring allows the solenoid to switch contacts and routes the power in another direction, allowing current to flow to the starter motor. In essence, the solenoid is a remote controlled switch used to direct current and is controlled by turning the car key in the ignition switch.

FOR YOUR FOLDER

1. What are the two main components in the starting system?
2. What is the function of the starter motor?
3. Why is the flywheel toothed?
4. How does the flywheel improve the performance of an engine?
5. What is a solenoid?
6. What is the distributor and how does it work?
7. How does the solenoid work?
8. How is the flywheel connected to the crankshaft?

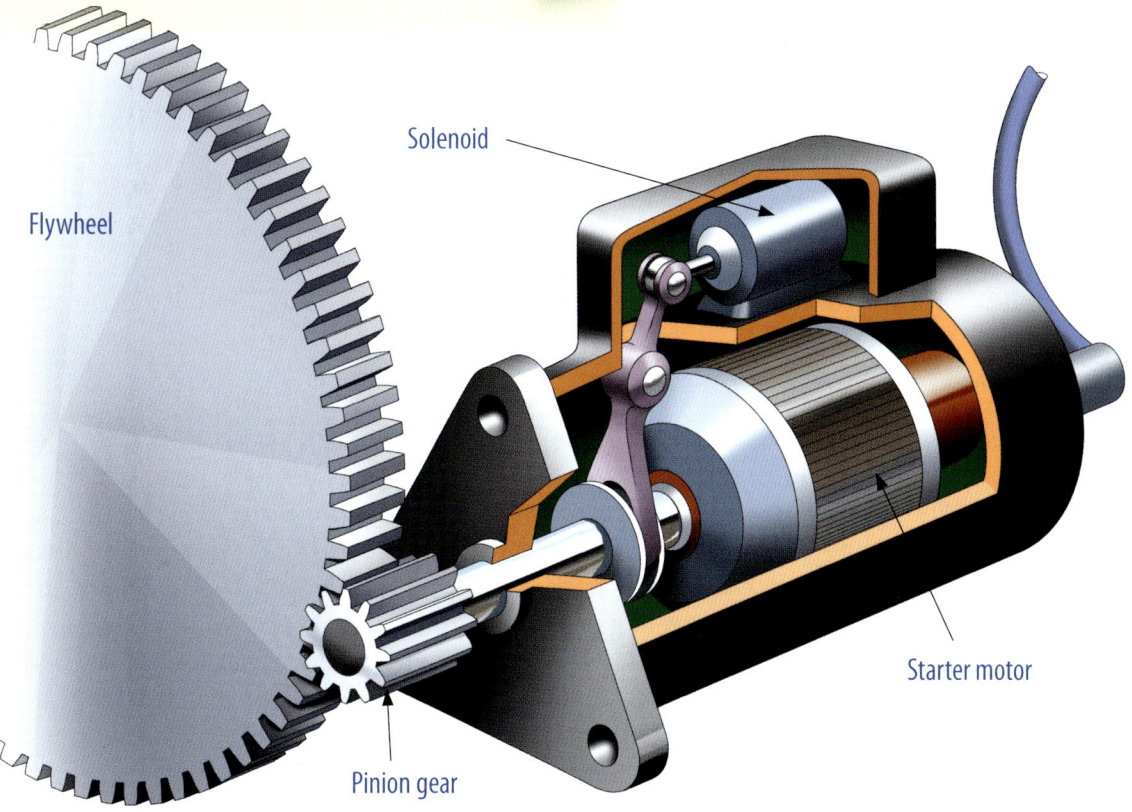

POWER UNITS

MAIN PARTS OF THE ENGINE

The following main components are shown in the diagrams on this page and the next.

Connecting rod
The connecting rod joins the piston to the crankshaft.

Gudgeon pin
The gudgeon pin connects the connecting rod to the piston.

Crankshaft
The crankshaft is turned by the flywheel and causes the pistons to move up and down.

Crank
The crank is the 90 degree bend in the shaft.

Crankpin
The crankpin is used to attach the connecting rod to the crankshaft.

Camshaft
The camshaft is connected by a timing chain to the crankshaft. As it rotates it controls springs that open and close the inlet and exhaust valves.

Sump
The sump is a tank at the very bottom of the engine that stores the oil used for lubrication of the cylinders and other engine parts.

How the engine works

The cylinder block and crankcase are the largest parts of the engine. Inside the cylinder block are four cylinders. The spark plugs are located at the top of each cylinder.

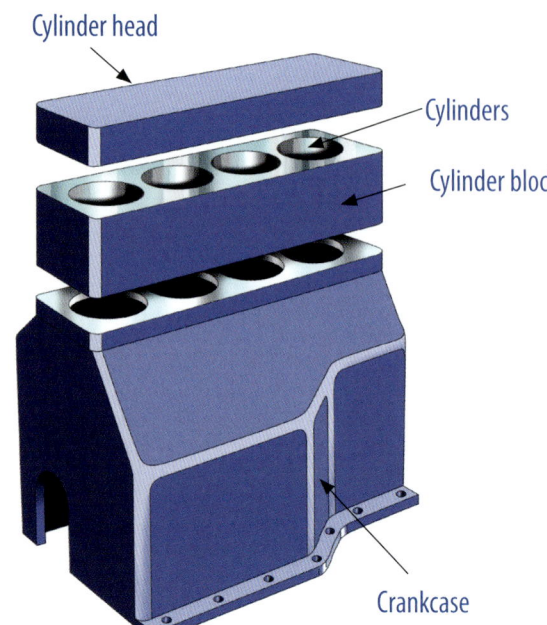

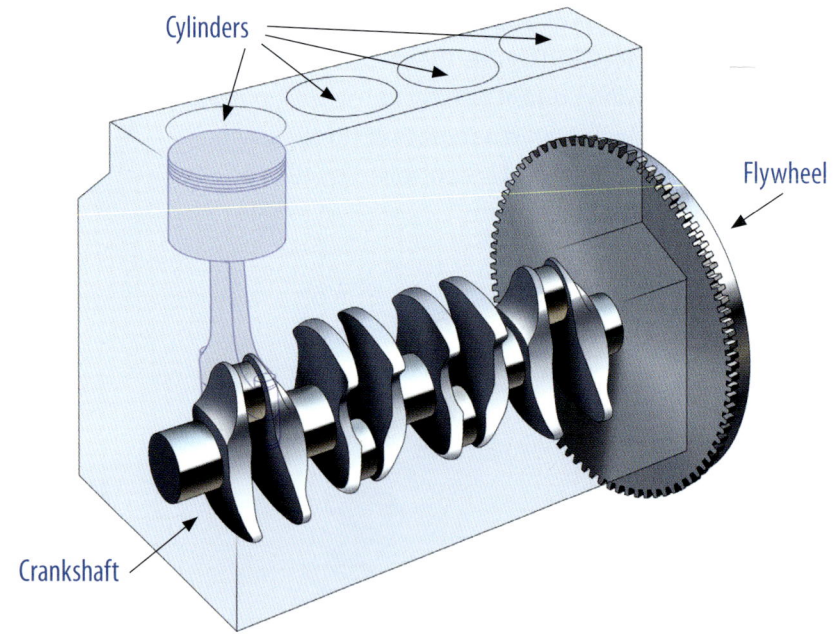

The cylinders are tubes, very accurately formed to allow the four pistons to slide up and down precisely and freely. A cylinder head sits on top of the cylinder block to cover the pistons. Whenever the starter motor 'starts', the large flywheel turns, causing the pistons to move up and down in a reciprocating motion. This causes the crankshaft, to which the pistons are connected, to turn round in a circular motion (rotary motion). This turning motion is transferred to the gearbox to set a vehicle in motion when the clutch is pressed and a gear selected. As the pistons are moving up and down petrol is pumped from the petrol tank to each of the cylinders. An inlet valve opens to allow the fuel into the cylinder, where the spark plug ignites the fuel when it is compressed. When a spark is created and the fuel ignited an explosion occurs, forcing the pistons back down at great speed to turn the crankshaft. As the pistons move up and down this process continually repeats itself.

The piston has three rings. The two top rings provide a gas tight seal to prevent any fuel from passing down either side of the piston and to ensure that compression of the fuel can be achieved. The bottom piston ring holds oil in place to lubricate the sides of the cylinder, allowing the pistons to slide freely up and down.

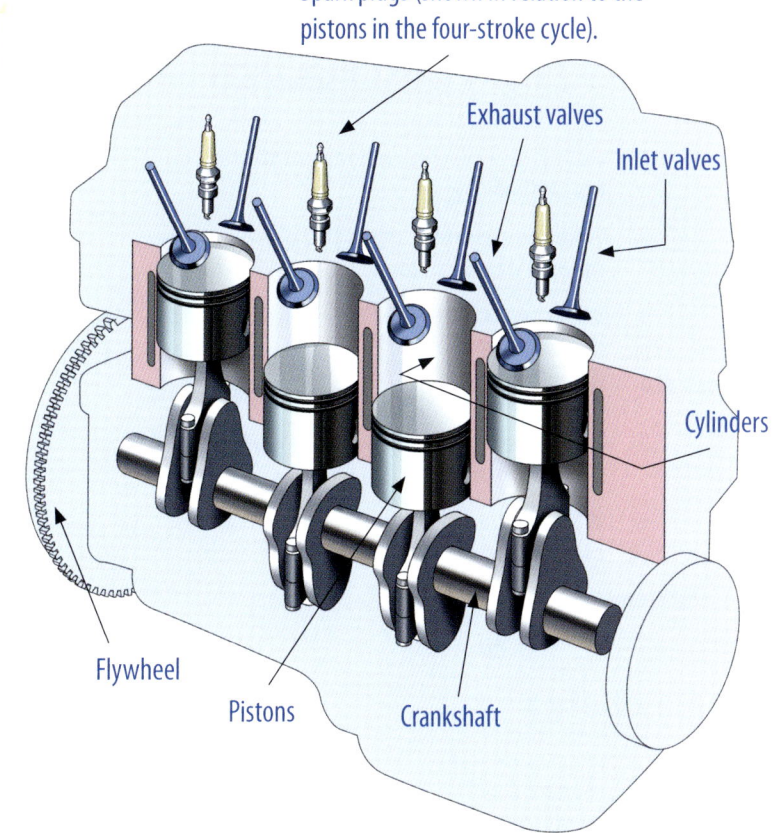

Spark plugs (shown in relation to the pistons in the four-stroke cycle).

Exhaust valves
Inlet valves
Cylinders
Flywheel
Pistons
Crankshaft

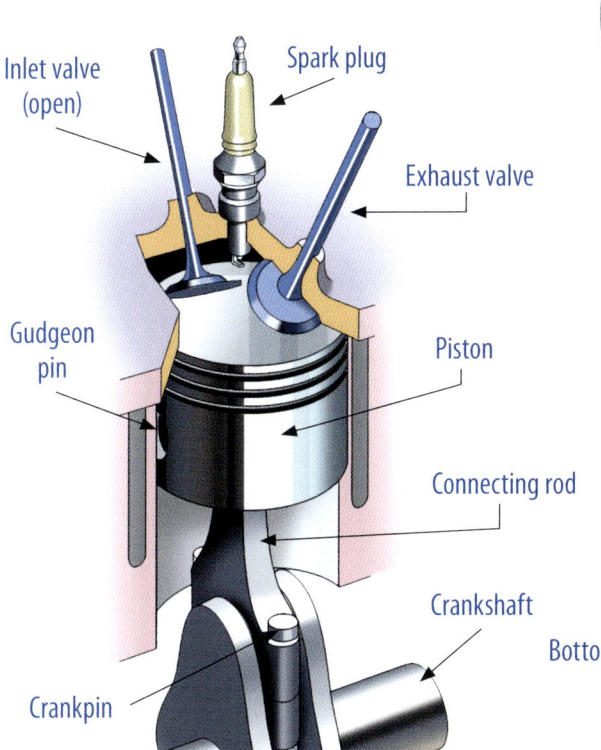

Inlet valve (open)
Spark plug
Exhaust valve
Gudgeon pin
Piston
Connecting rod
Crankshaft
Crankpin

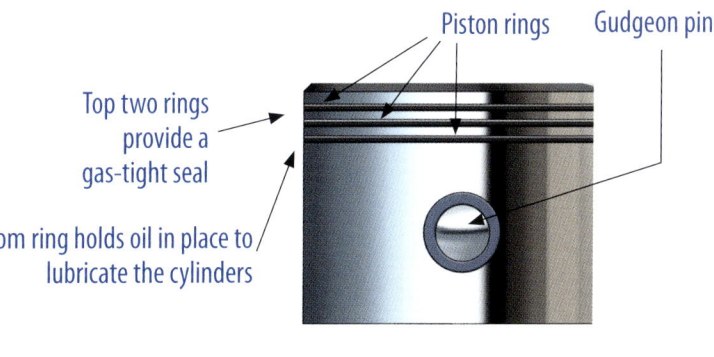

Piston rings
Gudgeon pin
Top two rings provide a gas-tight seal
Bottom ring holds oil in place to lubricate the cylinders

A timing chain is connected from the crankshaft to the camshaft. The timing chain enables the camshaft to control valve springs for opening and closing inlet and exhaust valves at the precise intervals needed. Inlet valves open to allow the fuel to flow into the cylinders to be ignited while the exhaust valves allow the burnt gases to flow into the exhaust pipe.

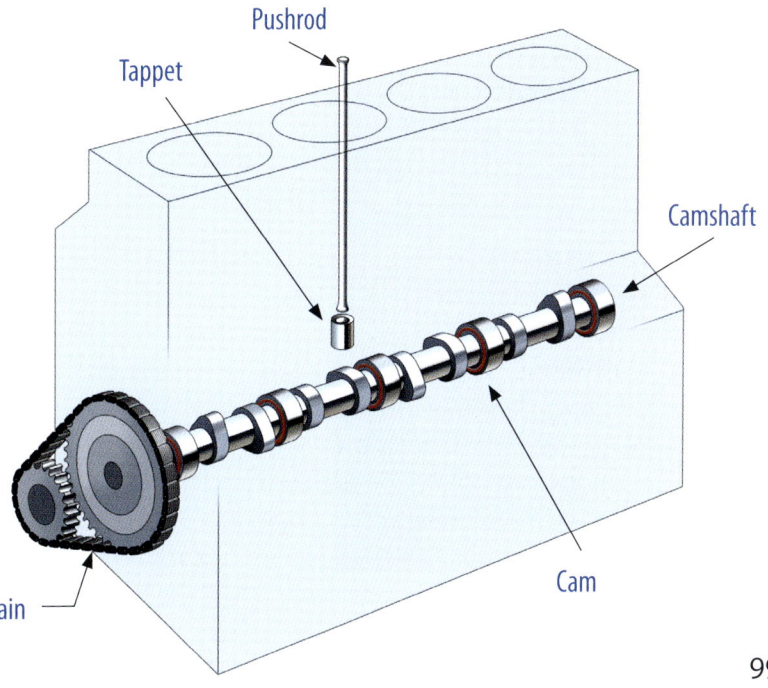

Pushrod
Tappet
Camshaft
Cam
Timing chain

FOR YOUR FOLDER

1. How is the piston connected to the crankshaft?
2. What component does the piston move up and down inside?
3. What two components are attached to the connecting rod?
4. What is the function of the gudgeon pin?
5. What is the function of the two top piston rings?
6. What is the function of the bottom piston ring?

FOR YOUR FOLDER

7. Why does the side of the cylinder need to be lubricated with oil?
8. Where is the cylinder head found?
9. What are the cylinders?
10. What is the function of the timing chain?
11. What two components form the largest part of the engine?
12. What two components is the timing chain connected to?

INTERNAL COMBUSTION ENGINES

There are three types of reciprocating internal combustion engines:

- The spark ignition four-stroke combustion cycle.
- The spark ignition two-stroke combustion cycle.
- The compression ignition four-stroke cycle (diesel engine).

These three engines all have one thing in common: they all convert reciprocating motion to rotary motion. In each cylinder the piston moves up and down in linear motion, causing the crankshaft, to which the pistons are connected, to turn in reciprocating motion. This turning motion is then transferred to the gearbox.

THE FOUR-STROKE CYCLE
(The spark-ignition four-stroke cycle)

The following four stages repeatedly take place in order:

1: Induction

The piston moves down in the cylinder. Springs attached to the camshaft open the inlet valve to allow the fuel into the cylinder.

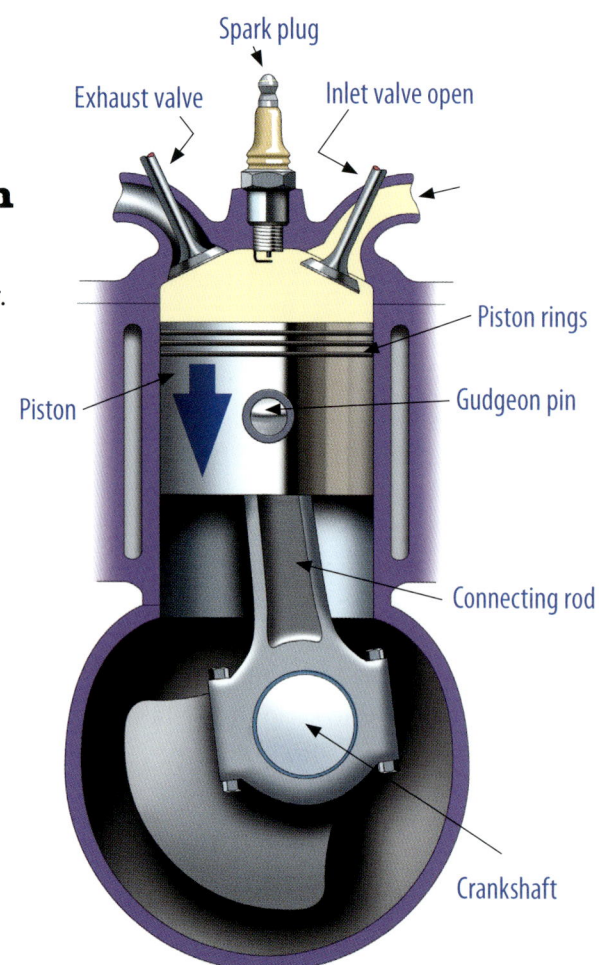

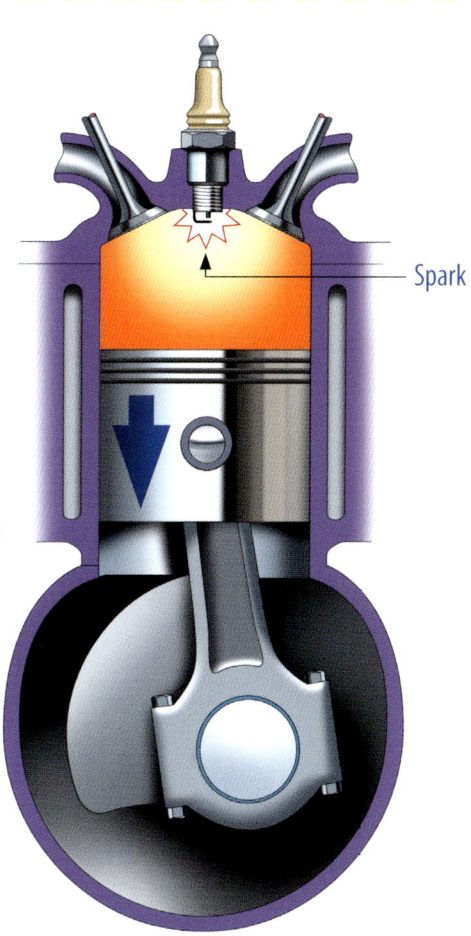

2: Compression

The piston moves up with both valves closed. The fuel is compressed in this tight space.

3: Power

When the piston is at the top and the petrol and air mixture is compressed, the spark plug ignites the fuel, causing an explosion and forcing the piston down again.

4: Exhaust

As the piston moves up, the exhaust valve opens via springs to allow burnt gasses to escape out into the exhaust pipe.

The four-stroke cycle then begins again.

FOR YOUR FOLDER

1. What are the four main stages of the four-stroke cycle?
2. During which stage will the spark plug ignite?
3. Briefly explain how the four-stroke cycle works.
4. On what stroke will the inlet valve open?
5. On what stroke will the exhaust valve open?
6. What component causes the inlet valve and exhaust valve to open?
7. What is the name of the component that the piston moves up and down inside?
8. What happens when the mixture of air and petrol burns rapidly on the power stroke?

THE TWO-STROKE CYCLE
(The spark-ignition two-stroke cycle)

Two-stroke engines are much smaller, lighter and cheaper than four-stroke engines. They have no valves like that of a four-stroke and therefore their operation is much simpler. Two-stroke engines are commonly used in lawnmowers, chainsaws and mopeds.

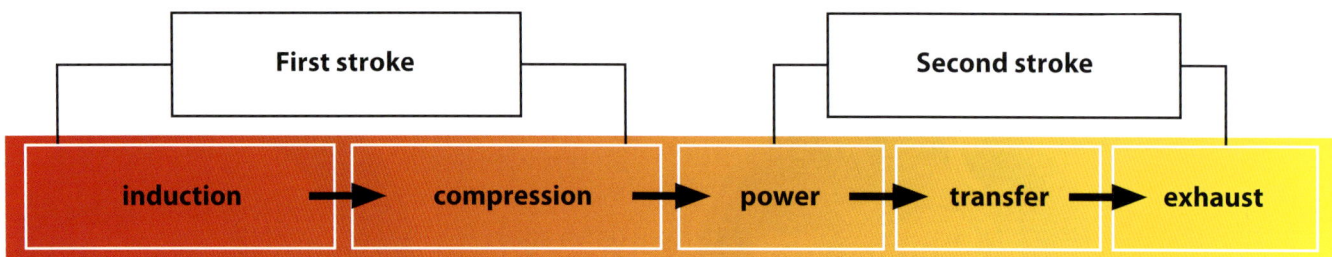

1: Induction and compression

As the piston moves up the cylinder the inlet valve is uncovered to allow fuel to flow into the cylinder. The piston compresses the fuel from the previous cycle and the spark plug ignites. This causes an explosion, forcing the piston back down.

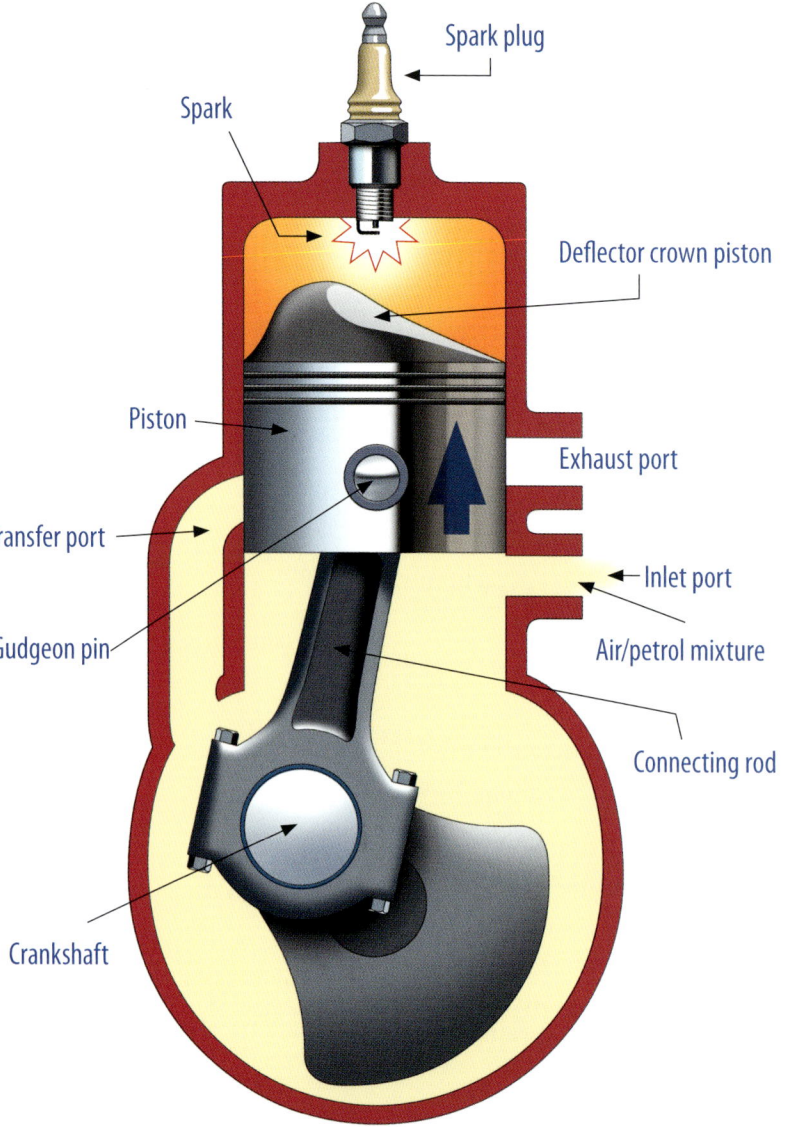

2: Power, transfer and exhaust

The piston moves down after the explosion, uncovering the exhaust port and the transfer port. As the fuel flows out of the transfer port to the top side of the piston, it pushes the burnt gases out through the exhaust port. The two-stroke cycle then begins again.

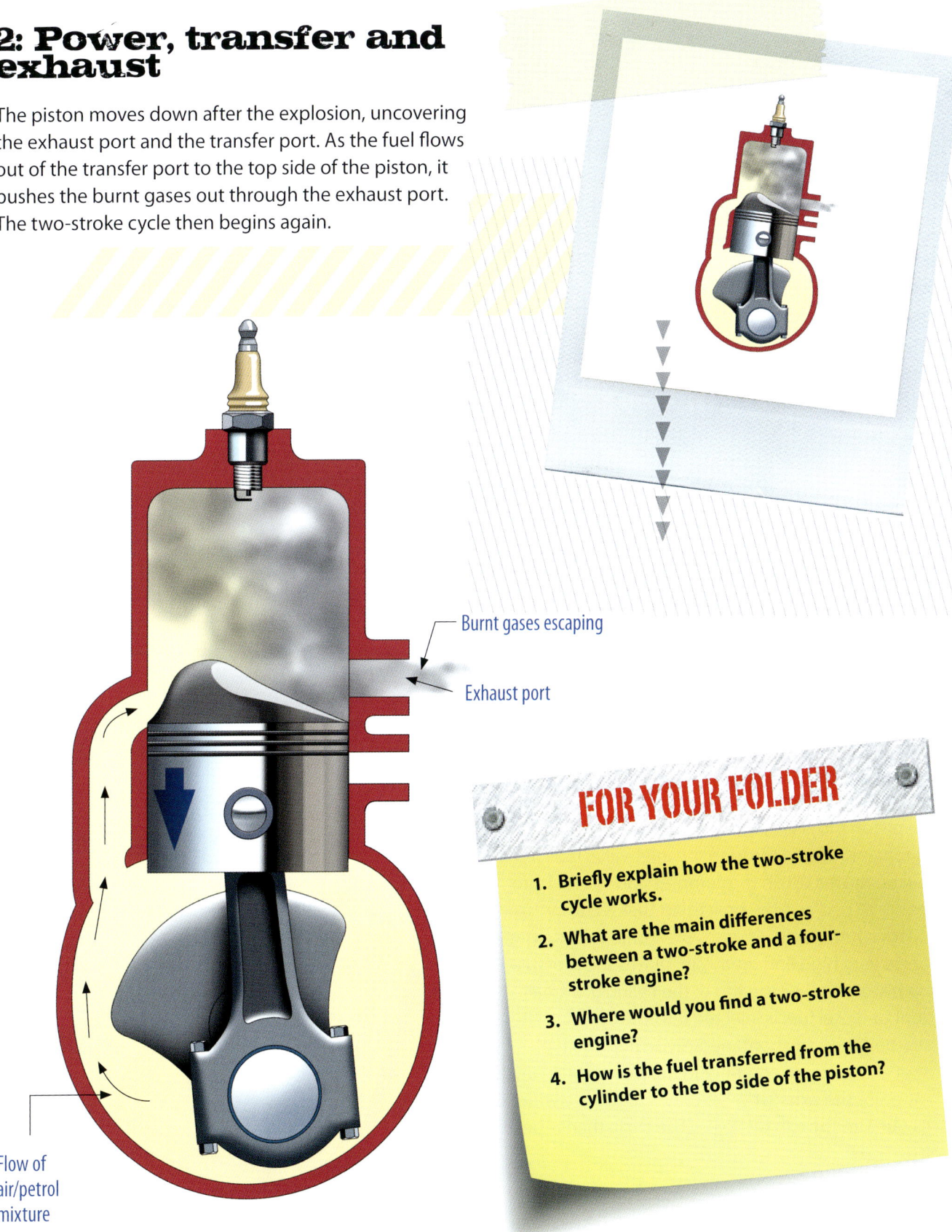

Burnt gases escaping

Exhaust port

Flow of air/petrol mixture

FOR YOUR FOLDER

1. Briefly explain how the two-stroke cycle works.
2. What are the main differences between a two-stroke and a four-stroke engine?
3. Where would you find a two-stroke engine?
4. How is the fuel transferred from the cylinder to the top side of the piston?

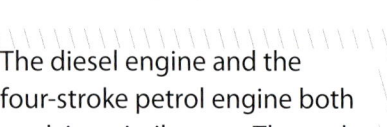

THE DIESEL ENGINE
(The compression-ignition four-stroke cycle)

The diesel engine and the four-stroke petrol engine both work in a similar way. The cycles are nearly the same. The main difference is that a diesel engine does not use spark plugs.

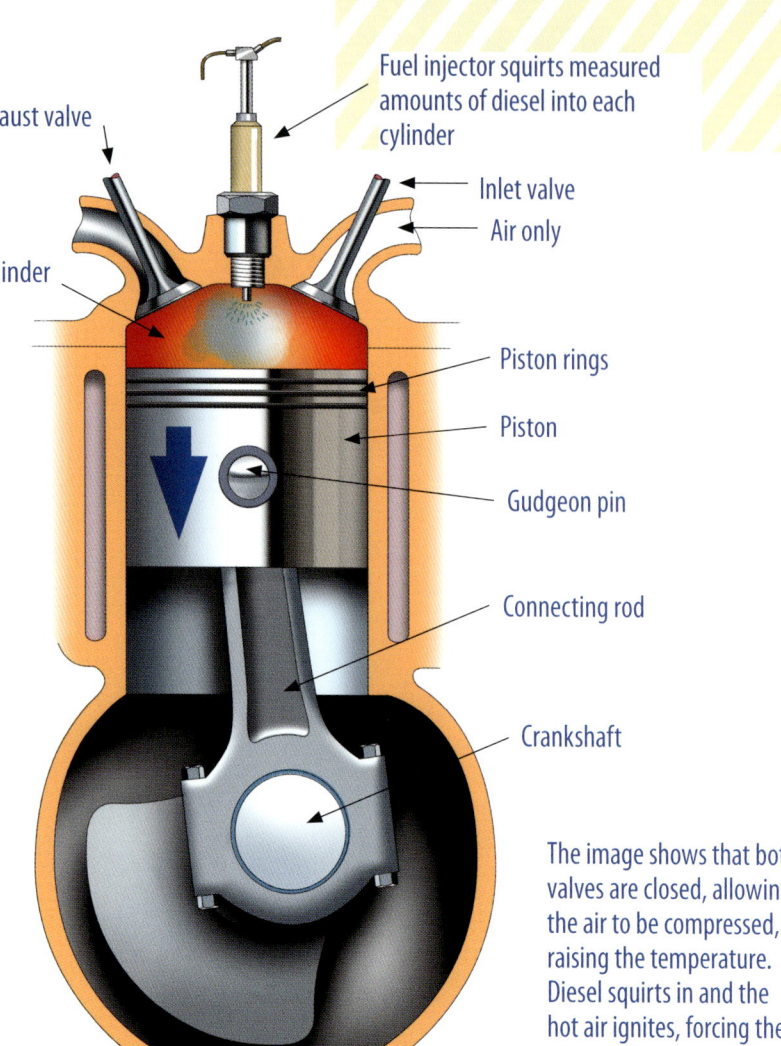

The image shows that both valves are closed, allowing the air to be compressed, raising the temperature. Diesel squirts in and the hot air ignites, forcing the pistons down.

induction, air only → compression, injection of fuel → power → exhaust

As the piston moves on the down stroke, the only thing that is drawn in through the inlet valve is air. As the piston moves up on the compression stroke, both valves are closed and the only thing that is compressed is air. This compressed air raises the temperature, which becomes very high and greatly increases the pressure. As the piston reaches the top of the cylinder, a small amount of diesel fuel is injected into the cylinder. The hot, compressed air spontaneously ignites the fuel, causing an explosion and forcing the piston back down. At this point the exhaust valve opens to allow all burnt gases out into the exhaust pipe. The cycle then repeats itself.

FOR YOUR FOLDER

1. What are the four cycles of a diesel engine?
2. What is the difference between the induction stroke of a diesel and that of a petrol four-stroke engine?
3. Why is the air temperature very high in a diesel engine?
4. How is the fuel ignited in a diesel engine?
5. How does the fuel get into the cylinder?
6. Draw a block diagram to show the cycles of a diesel engine.
7. Name the stroke defined by the piston moving up with both valves closed.

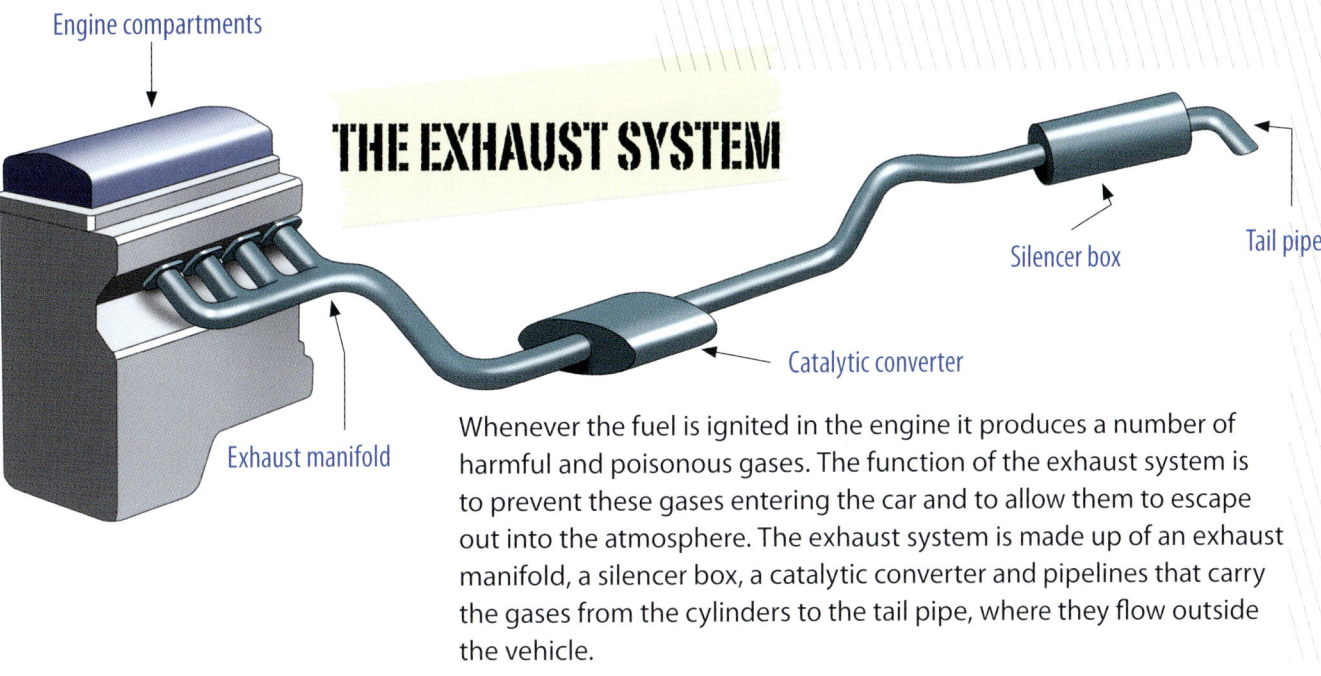

THE EXHAUST SYSTEM

Whenever the fuel is ignited in the engine it produces a number of harmful and poisonous gases. The function of the exhaust system is to prevent these gases entering the car and to allow them to escape out into the atmosphere. The exhaust system is made up of an exhaust manifold, a silencer box, a catalytic converter and pipelines that carry the gases from the cylinders to the tail pipe, where they flow outside the vehicle.

The manifold

The manifold collects all the burnt gases from each of the four cylinders into one pipe.

The silencer box or damper

Whenever the fuel is ignited the burnt gases expand and produce sound waves in the airflow. This airflow causes a lot of noise outside the engine and is considered a form of noise pollution. This noise can be reduced through the use of a silencer box (shown below). The silencer box contains baffles, which the air has to move around. This slows down the air and results in reduced gas pressure and noise.

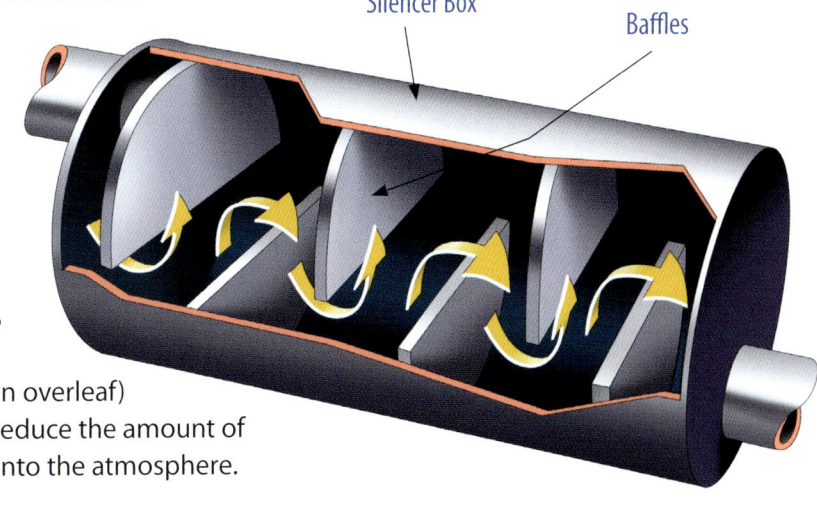

Gases

The gases produced by the engine include carbon monoxide, sulphur dioxide, lead, oxides of nitrogen, carbon dioxide, and hydrocarbons.

Catalytic converter

Most modern cars have these converters (shown overleaf) fitted on the exhaust pipe. Their function is to reduce the amount of harmful and poisonous emissions allowed out into the atmosphere.

Diesel particulate filter

A diesel particulate filter does a similar job to the catalytic converter. It is fitted to diesel vehicles to capture and store exhaust soot to help reduce emissions from diesel engines. A liquid, known by the brand name *AdBlue*, can also be added to diesel cars to help reduce the harmful emissions they create.

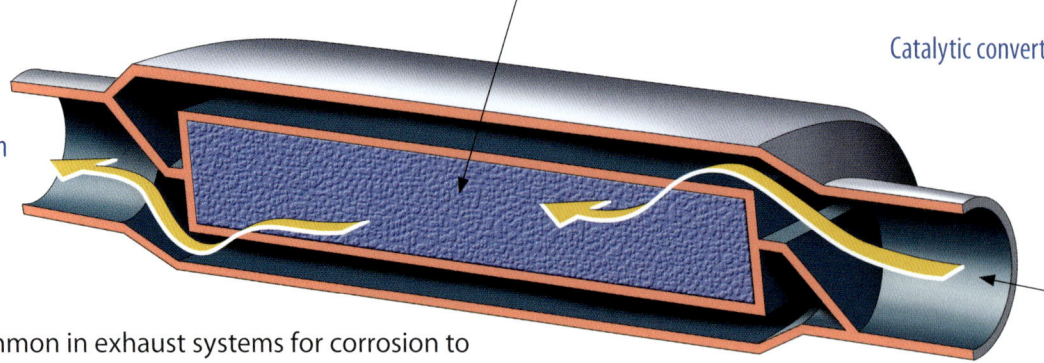

Chamber of ceramic molecules that react with and eliminate certain harmful emissions

Catalytic converter

Fewer harmful gasses exposed in the atmosphere

Flow of exhaust gases

It is quite common in exhaust systems for corrosion to occur, especially as all the exhaust pipes are underneath the vehicle. These pipes can occasionally strike a hump if a vehicle is driven over an uneven road surface or driven carelessly. If a vehicle drives through a puddle or a flooded road the exhaust system will get wet and may take a long time to dry out because the underneath of a vehicle is rarely exposed to sunlight. Rusting or damage to the pipes can cause holes, causing gas to leak out before passing through the silencer box, damper and catalytic converter, making the exhaust noisy. The exhaust pipes, silencer box and catalytic converter should be rigidly mounted to the underneath of the vehicle. If these mountings become loose, allowing the exhaust pipe to drop, it is likely to strike the road, further damaging the exhaust system. The exhaust system's mounting should be regularly checked to ensure it is secure. This will avoid any unnecessary damage and expensive replacements. If parts of the exhaust system are loose, you should take your vehicle to a mechanic to secure the problem part.

FOR YOUR FOLDER

1. What is the function of the exhaust system?
2. Explain what a manifold does.
3. What is the name of the component that helps to reduce the noise of a vehicle?
4. How does this component work?
5. What is the function of a catalytic converter?
6. Name the component that attaches the exhaust to the engine.
7. Make a list of exhaust gases.

THE FUEL SYSTEM

The fuel needed to drive a petrol car is a mixture of petrol and air. The petrol is normally stored in a tank at the back of the car and flows to the engine through connecting pipelines. Petrol is made from crude oil.

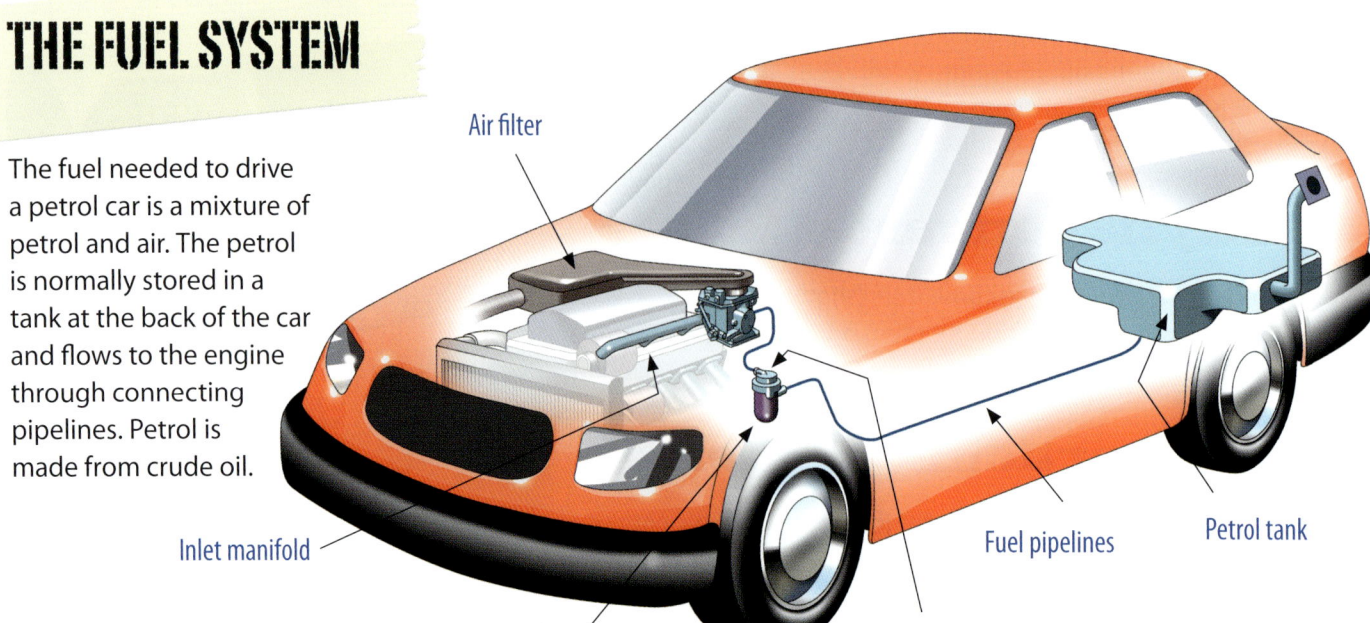

Air filter

Inlet manifold

Petrol pump

Fuel filter

Fuel pipelines

Petrol tank

106

These pipes are usually fitted underneath the car, so the fuel, which is under pressure, needs to be pumped up into the engine by a pump. The petrol is mixed with air as it passes through the inlet manifold and it is this mixture that is to be ignited in the cylinders by the spark plugs. The mixture is then distributed to each individual cylinder through inlet valves, via a fuel injector (shown below right). The injector sprays the fuel into the top of the cylinder like a fine mist.

A fuel filter is used to ensure only clean fuel gets into the inlet manifold, as any particle of dust or dirt could cause a blockage and restrict the flow of fuel. The air is taken in from the atmosphere and may contain dirt or dust particles that could clog or block moving parts in the engine. An air filter is in place to prevent these particles getting through into the fuel, allowing only clean air to pass.

It is important to get both fuel and air filters changed regularly as they will become clogged up with dirt and dust. It is also important to check a vehicle's fuel system for leaks. A parked vehicle that develops a wet patch beneath could indicate a leak, as could any wetness underneath the bonnet. You should always avoid naked lights around a vehicle's engine compartment, as fuel can easily catch fire or cause an explosion, and you may not see or notice a leak until it is too late.

The function of the inlet manifold is to deliver the fuel to the injectors which then distributes the fuel to the individual cylinders. The fuel injection system is an economical system as it only uses measured amounts of fuel, determined by how the vehicle is being driven. The fuel injection system has two main advantages:

- It is not wasteful of fuel and only uses measured amounts.
- Long-term it saves money because the fuel lasts longer and the car covers more miles.

Older vehicles may use a carburettor instead of fuel injectors. The carburettor mixes the petrol and air together which becomes the fuel. The fuel then travels from the carburettor to the inlet manifold. The carburettor is discussed in more depth on page 108.

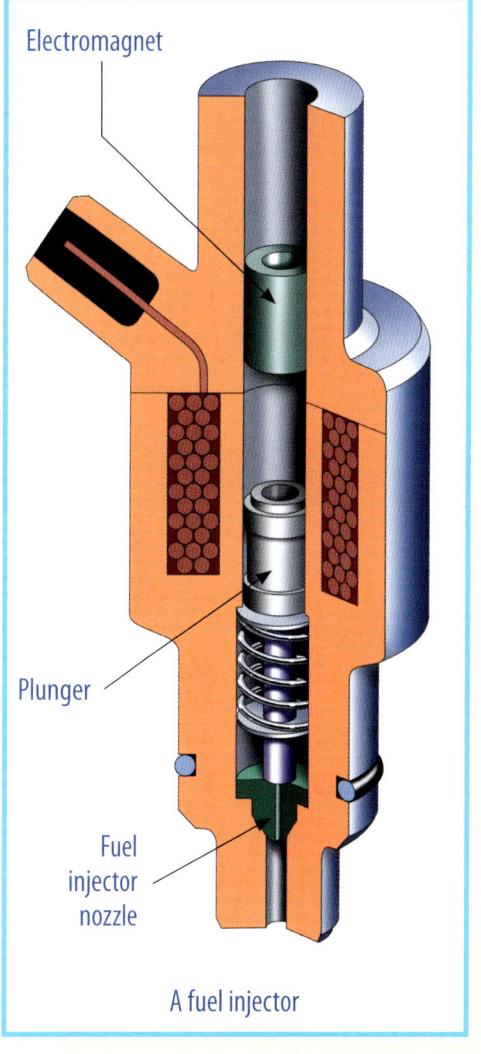

A fuel injector

FOR YOUR FOLDER

1. What is the fuel for making a vehicle move made from?
2. Where is the fuel stored?
3. How is petrol raised up to the inlet manifold?
4. List the main parts of the fuel system.
5. What is the function of the inlet manifold?
6. Why does an air filter need to be fitted?
7. Briefly explain how the fuel injection system works.
8. List two advantages of the fuel injection system.

The carburettor

The carburettor was used in the past before fuel injectors became universal. A carburettor has two main functions:

- To mix the correct amounts of petrol and air together to make the fuel for burning in cylinders.
- To control the amount of fuel sent to each cylinder.

Petrol flows from the tank at the back of the car, through a petrol pump, to a float chamber in the carburettor. This chamber ensures that there is a regular, continuous flow of petrol to be mixed with air. When the chamber fills up a float pushes a needle valve into the pipe to stop the flow from the petrol tank.

The venturi is the narrow part of the carburettor where the petrol and air mix for the first time. A jet is used to ease the inflow of petrol, creating a spray. The air flow then carries the petrol on through the throttle. Whenever the accelerator pedal is pressed the throttle valve opens to allow fuel into the cylinders. The harder the accelerator pedal is pressed the wider the throttle valve opens to allow more fuel into the cylinders. The fuel then flows to the inlet manifold, which distributes a specific amount of fuel to each of the four cylinders. The inlet valve will open on the induction stroke, allowing the fuel into each cylinder.

FOR YOUR FOLDER

1. What is the function of the carburettor?
2. What is the function of the float in the float chamber?
3. What is the venturi?
4. What is the function of the jet?
5. What happens when the accelerator pedal is pressed?

THE TRANSMISSION SYSTEM

The transmission system is used to set a vehicle moving. Its main parts are as shown below:

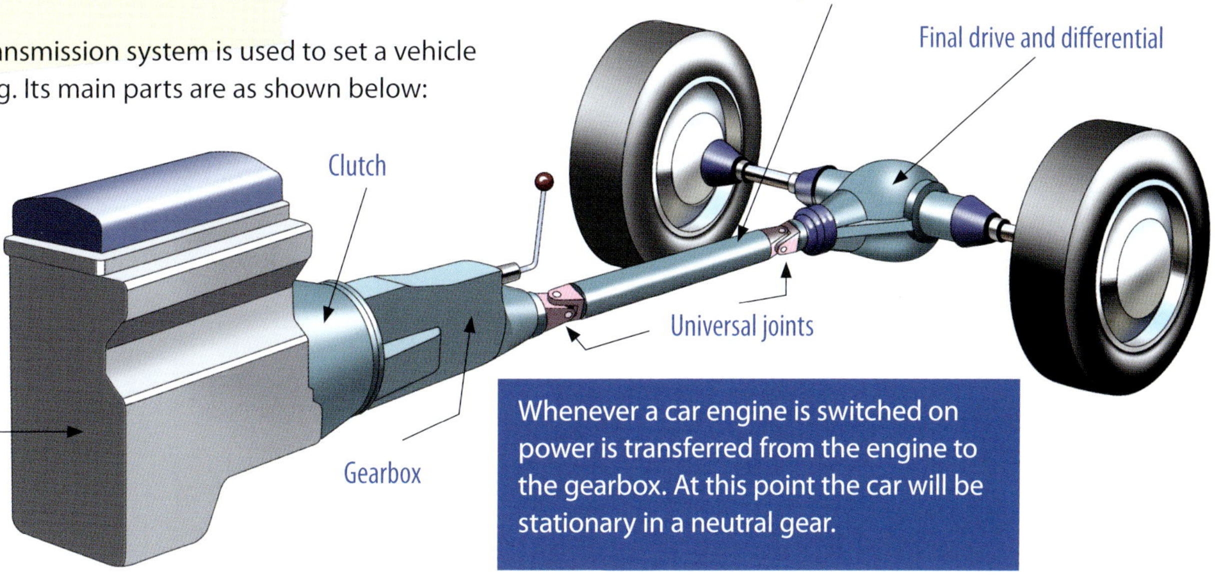

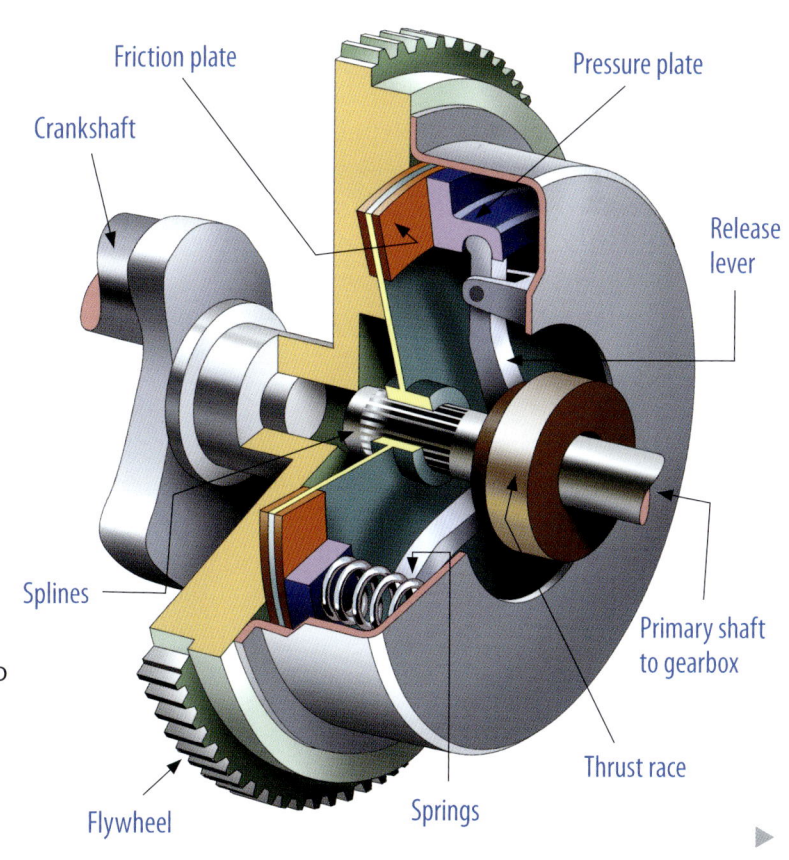

Whenever a car engine is switched on power is transferred from the engine to the gearbox. At this point the car will be stationary in a neutral gear.

| The clutch | → | The gearbox | → | The propeller shaft and universal joints | → | The final drive and differential |

Although the car is stationary, all the gears inside the gearbox will be rotating. To select a gear, in order to move the vehicle, the gears have to be stopped for a moment. This is achieved by pressing the clutch pedal, which disengages the engine from the gearbox, stopping all the gears. The gear stick can then be moved to select an appropriate gear. By moving the foot off the clutch pedal the engine is re-engaged and the vehicle will start to move.

The clutch

The main function of the dry friction clutch is to engage (connect) and disengage (disconnect) the engine from the gearbox. By doing this an appropriate gear can be selected.

109

▶ The primary shaft has splines carved into it in certain places to enable the friction plate to slide along the shaft. This slide allows the plate to be either forced tight against, or moved away from, the flywheel. When the clutch is engaged, which is most of the time, the friction plate is forced tight against the flywheel by springs on a pressure plate. The flywheel causes the primary shaft to rotate through to the gearbox.

To disengage the engine from the gearbox the clutch pedal must be pressed and held in. In so doing this, a linkage mechanism pulls the thrust race, which is connected to the pressure plate. The springs are then compressed allowing the friction plate to move away from the flywheel. When this happens the primary shaft will stop rotating as will the gears in the gearbox.

Upon releasing the clutch pedal the linkage mechanism releases the springs, which push the pressure plate back against the friction plate, forcing it tight against the flywheel. The primary shaft will once again rotate, as will the gears in the gearbox.

The friction plate is made from metal as is the flywheel. The friction plate needs protected, so both sides of it are faced (covered) with a special material designed to reduce overheating and wear.

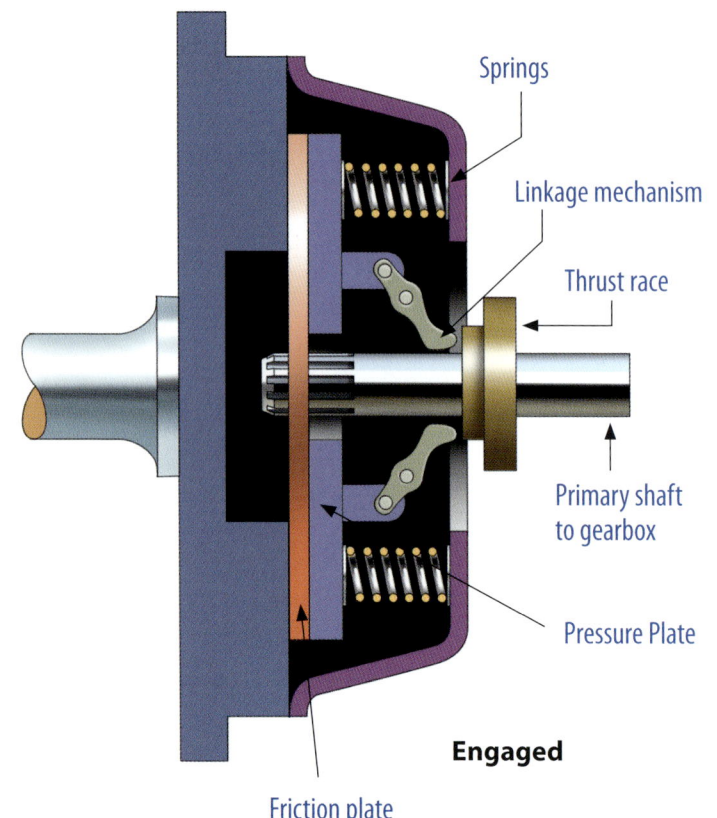

Engaged

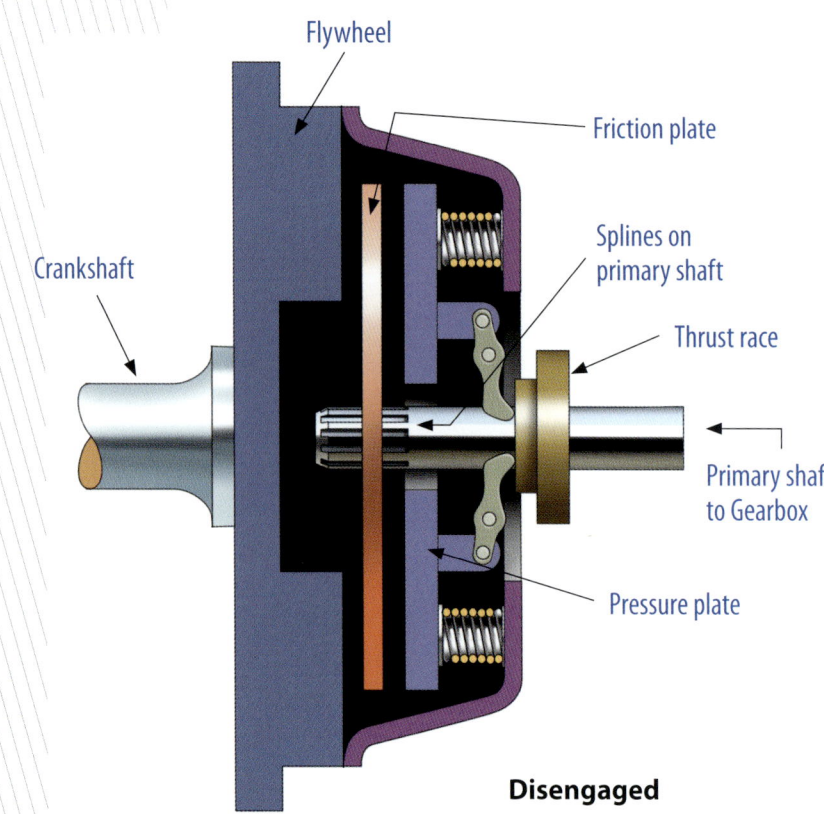

Disengaged

The gearbox

Most gearboxes have five forward gears and one reverse gear. The gearbox is designed to produce a range of speeds depending on where a vehicle is travelling. For example, high gears are used for increased speed when driving on the flat, whereas driving on an incline or in slow moving traffic require lower gears. Lubrication is essential within the transmission system and gearbox because of the large number of moving parts. This lubricating oil will not only ease the movement of parts but reduce friction, heat and wear.

When a vehicle is first switched on power is transmitted from the engine, through the clutch, to the gearbox, which is initially in a neutral gear. The primary shaft has one gear that continuously rotates and it is connected to the clutch. Below the primary shaft is a second shaft, the layshaft. When the clutch pedal is pressed by the driver's foot the primary shaft will stop rotating as will all the gears on the layshaft. The layshaft has a number of gears that are permanently fixed from reverse, to first, through to fifth. A third shaft, the main shaft, is mounted at the end of the primary shaft and carries power to the propellor shaft.

- Gear stick
- Selectors
- Bolted to universal joints connected to propeller shaft
- Dog clutch
- Main shaft
- Layshaft
- Primary shaft from clutch

How is a gear selected?

The main shaft has splines that allows gears to slide from side to side. The gear stick is connected to selectors and dog clutches that slide the gears along the main shaft to engage with gears on the layshaft. This can only happen if all the gears have momentarily been stopped rotating by the clutch, allowing specific gears to be engaged together.

Moving the gear stick without pushing the clutch in will result in a grinding sound and the toothed gear wheels could be damaged. The main shaft is connected to the propeller shaft which transmits the power and motion from the gearbox to the back wheels, which drive the car.

The diagrams below show how the layshaft and main shaft have different gears engaged to provide different speeds for the back wheels. For less speed and more power the gear wheel on the main shaft will be larger.

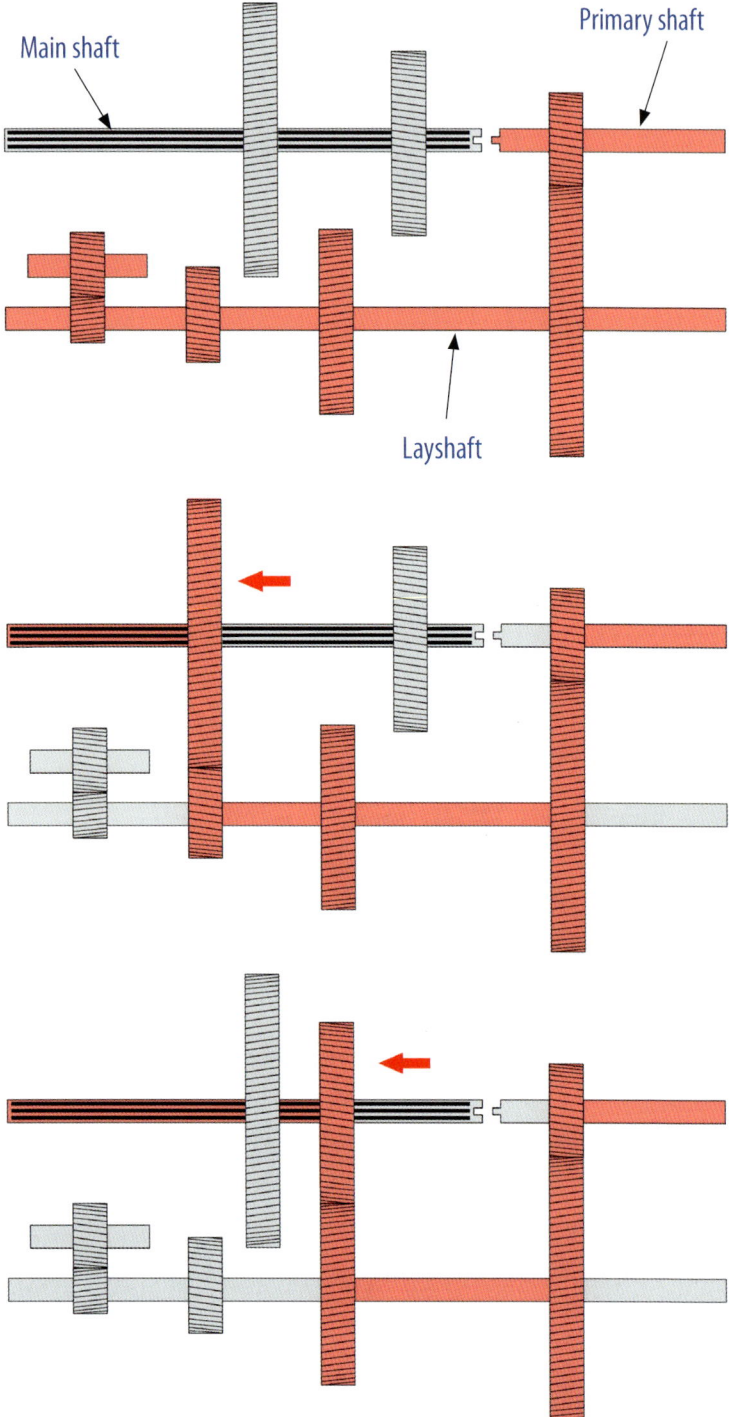

Neutral – The small gear on the primary shaft carries power from the engine, through the clutch, to the gearbox. This small gear is permanently meshed with a gear on the layshaft. The main shaft is not connected to the layshaft.

First gear – The large gear on the main shaft slides along the splines to mesh with first gear on the layshaft. This gear is designed for high power and a slow speed.

Second gear – This gear arrangement has slightly less power, with a slight increase in speed.

Third gear – With the need for more speed the main shaft is connected directly to the primary shaft.

Reverse gear – This uses an idler gear in the middle to turn the main shaft and the layshaft in the same direction, causing the car to move backwards.

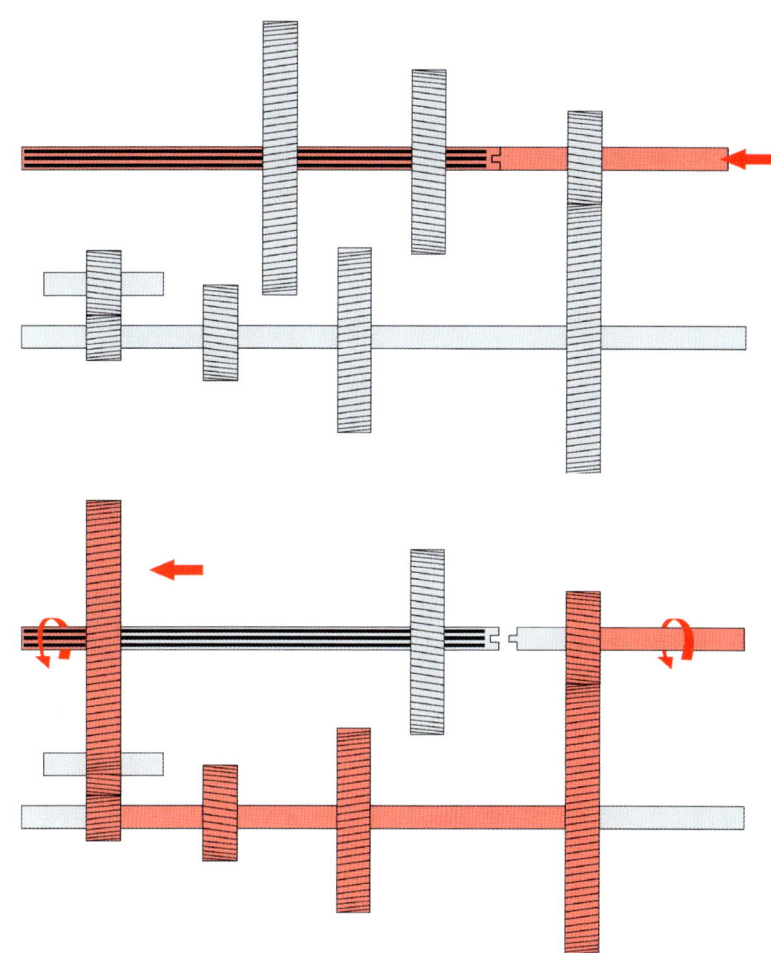

Calculating gear ratios

Gear ratios are used by vehicle manufacturers to work out either the torque (power) produced by the engine or the speeds at which the vehicle can travel. Gear ratios are determined by the relationship between the number of teeth that mesh together between two gears.

The calculation to work out gear ratios is very simple.

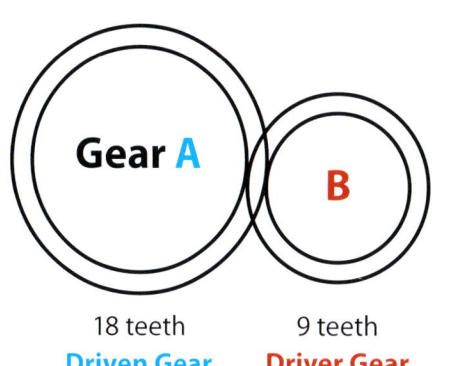

18 teeth **Driven Gear**   9 teeth **Driver Gear**

To calculate the gear ratio: **Gear ratio** = $\dfrac{\text{Number of teeth on driven gear}}{\text{Number of teeth on driver gear}}$

$$= \dfrac{18}{9} = \dfrac{2}{1}$$

Which is written as **Gear Ratio = 2:1**

113

Propeller shaft

The propeller shaft, also known as the drive shaft, is a hollow, steel tube. Connected to the main shaft in the gearbox, it carries power to the rear axle to make the vehicle move. The propeller shaft is fixed underneath the vehicle and needs to be flexible to adjust to the vehicle travelling over uneven road surfaces. If flexibility was not provided the propeller shaft could be severely damaged when the wheels bounce over a bump in the road. To allow for this flexibility the propeller shaft needs to be fitted at each end with universal joints.

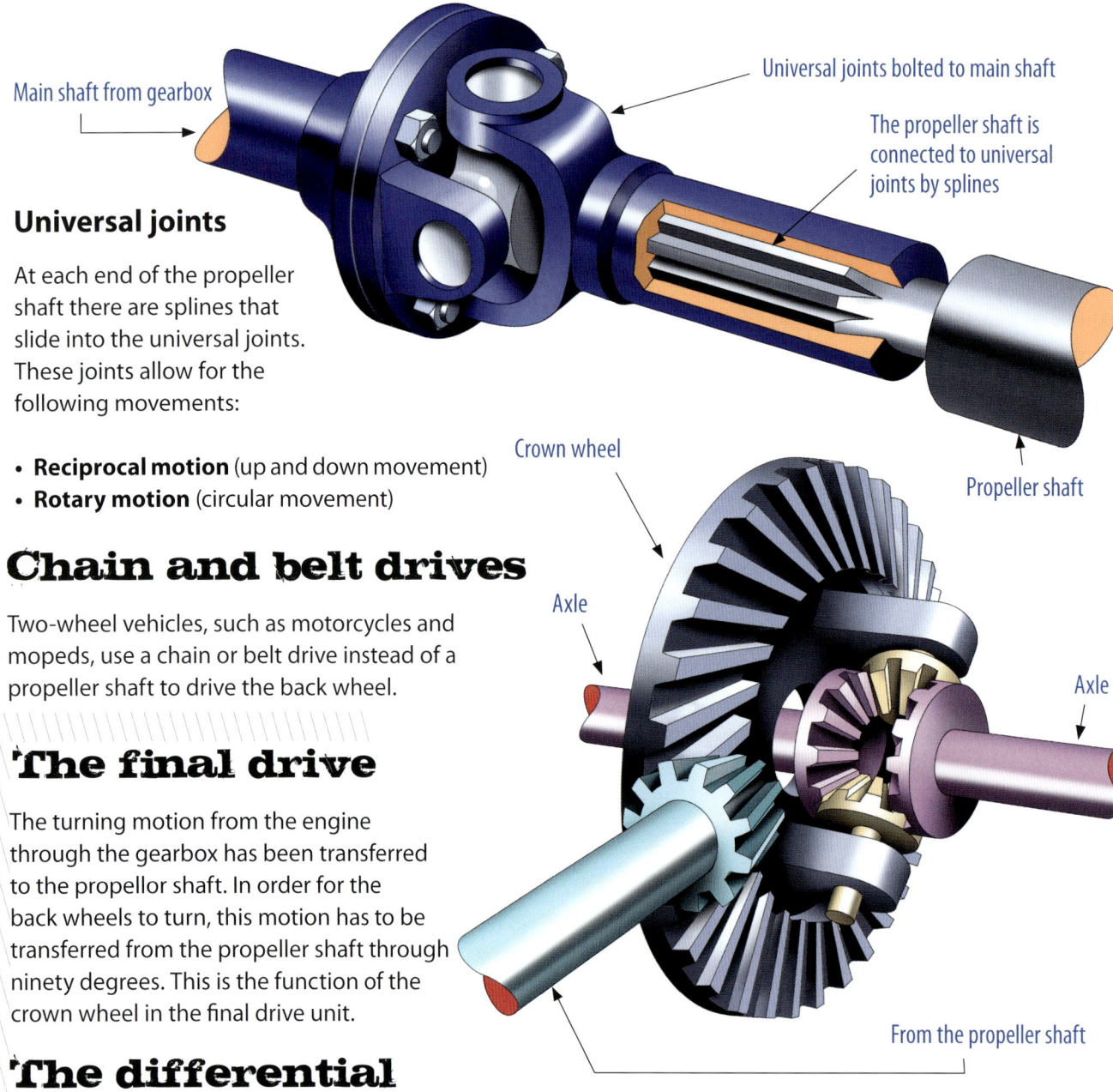

Universal joints

At each end of the propeller shaft there are splines that slide into the universal joints. These joints allow for the following movements:

- **Reciprocal motion** (up and down movement)
- **Rotary motion** (circular movement)

Chain and belt drives

Two-wheel vehicles, such as motorcycles and mopeds, use a chain or belt drive instead of a propeller shaft to drive the back wheel.

The final drive

The turning motion from the engine through the gearbox has been transferred to the propellor shaft. In order for the back wheels to turn, this motion has to be transferred from the propeller shaft through ninety degrees. This is the function of the crown wheel in the final drive unit.

The differential

Whenever a vehicle is travelling on a straight part of the road the two back wheels are turning at the same speed. However, when turning a corner, the outer wheel will have a greater distance to travel and will therefore need to turn faster than the inner wheel. The function of the differential is to allow one wheel to turn faster than the other. If this was not catered for, a vehicle could easily skid or lose control.

THE STEERING SYSTEM

The steering system is in place to allow the driver to control and manoeuvre the vehicle quickly and safely, at different speeds, in all directions.

Rack and pinion gear

A rack and pinion gear is used to control the steering of a vehicle. This simple steering arrangement has a small pinion gear attached to the lower end of the steering column that is turned by the steering wheel. The pinion gear sits on a toothed rack that is connected to the front wheels. On turning the steering wheel, the pinion gear moves the rack to the left or to the right causing the wheels to turn.

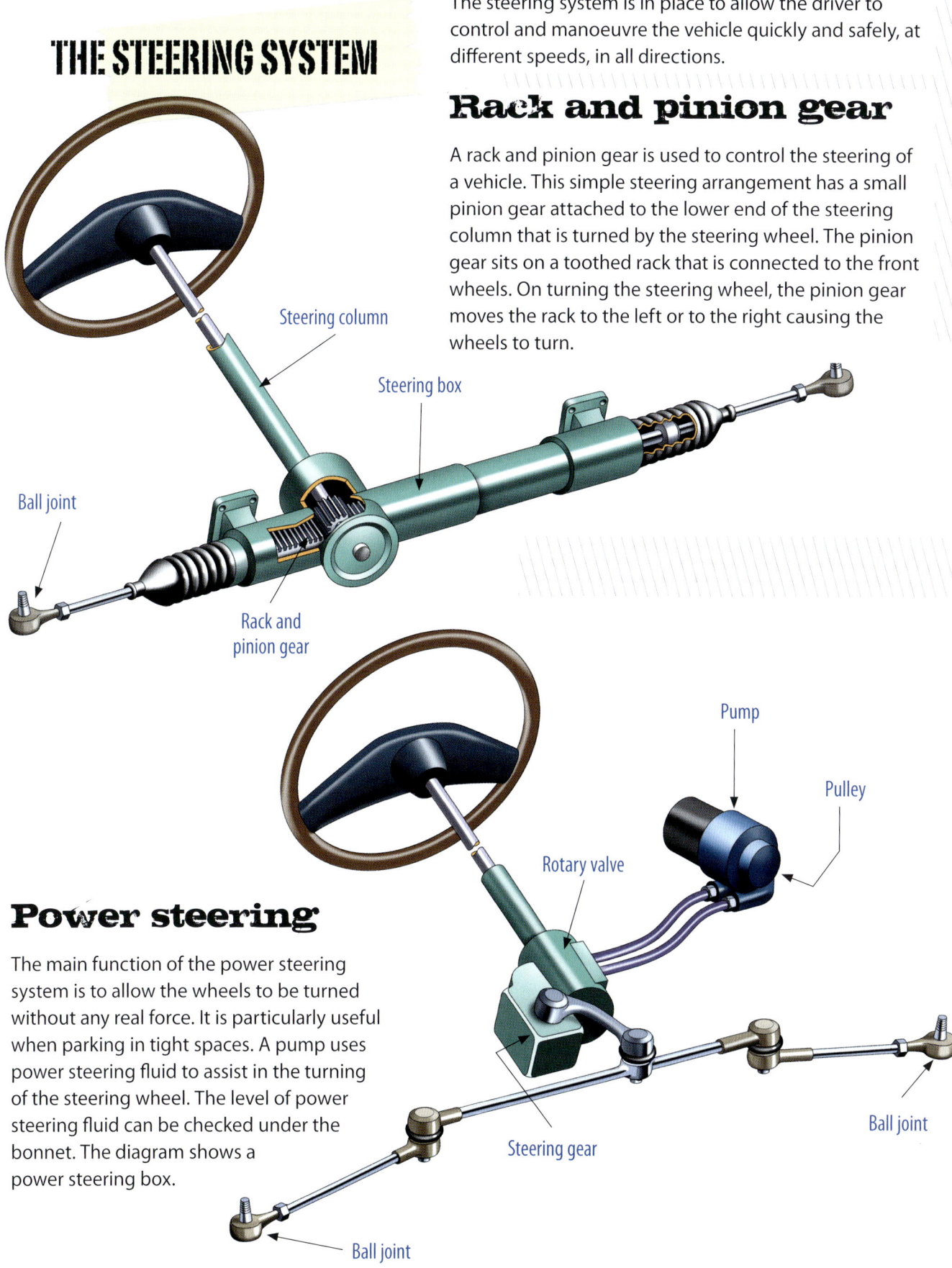

Power steering

The main function of the power steering system is to allow the wheels to be turned without any real force. It is particularly useful when parking in tight spaces. A pump uses power steering fluid to assist in the turning of the steering wheel. The level of power steering fluid can be checked under the bonnet. The diagram shows a power steering box.

115

THE SUSPENSION SYSTEM

When driving on the roads a vehicle will encounter bumps, humps, uneven road surfaces and sometimes potholes. Any of these can cause bounces or jolts. The function of the suspension system is to absorb these movements, allowing the vehicle and its occupants to remain safe and comfortable.

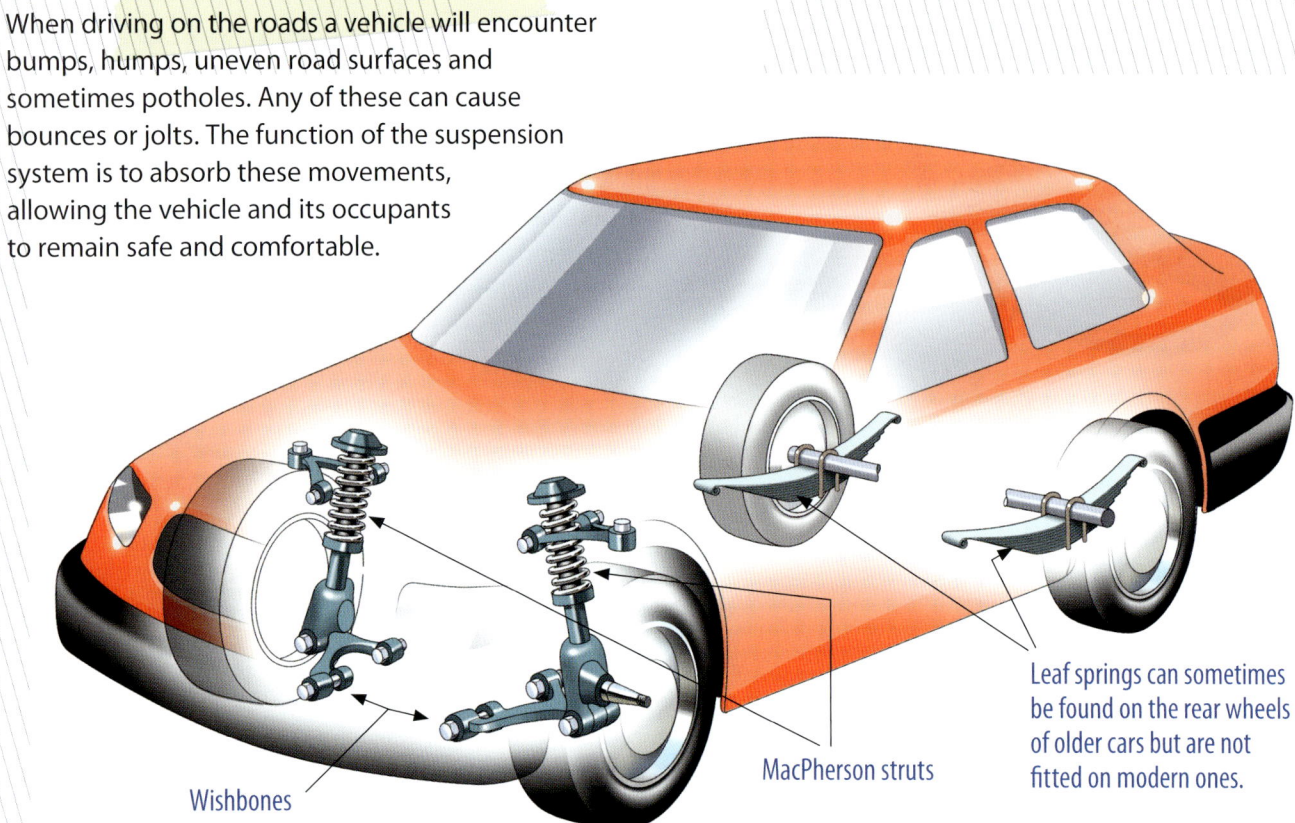

Wishbones

MacPherson struts

Leaf springs can sometimes be found on the rear wheels of older cars but are not fitted on modern ones.

Suspension systems should result in the following:

- A comfortable, even journey as the vehicle will absorb the effects of bounces or jolts.
- Less expense and maintenance for the vehicle owner caused by wear and tear, as the vehicle will be shaken less.
- Easier control and safer handling, because the wheels will always be in contact with the road.

A suspension system is made up of a number of different components for the front wheels and the back wheels.

Front wheel suspension

The function of a **coil spring** is to absorb the wheels' up-and-down movement. However, when compressed, a coil can spring back to its original shape at speed. This return action needs to be slowed down, otherwise the vehicle will repeatedly bounce up and down. The function of a shock absorber (damper) is to slow down the return of a spring.

The **MacPherson strut** is the most common front wheel suspension system. It is made up of a strut, a coil spring and a shock absorber. The strut takes the impact of the wheel striking something, while the shock absorbers slow down the movement of the impact. Each shock absorber uses a piston, which is connected to the suspension system and plunges down into a cylinder of oil, slowing down the movement.

Shock absorbers can be tested for efficiency by a simple bounce test. To carry out the bounce test you need to press down on each corner of your vehicle at a time. Your vehicle should push down and spring back up again. As it bounces back up it should rise above its starting point and then rest back to its original position. If it drops below this starting point the shock absorber needs replacing. It is important that this check is carried out on each corner.

Wishbones are a linkage mechanism connected from the car body to the wheels. Their function is to absorb jolts caused by a wheel striking something.

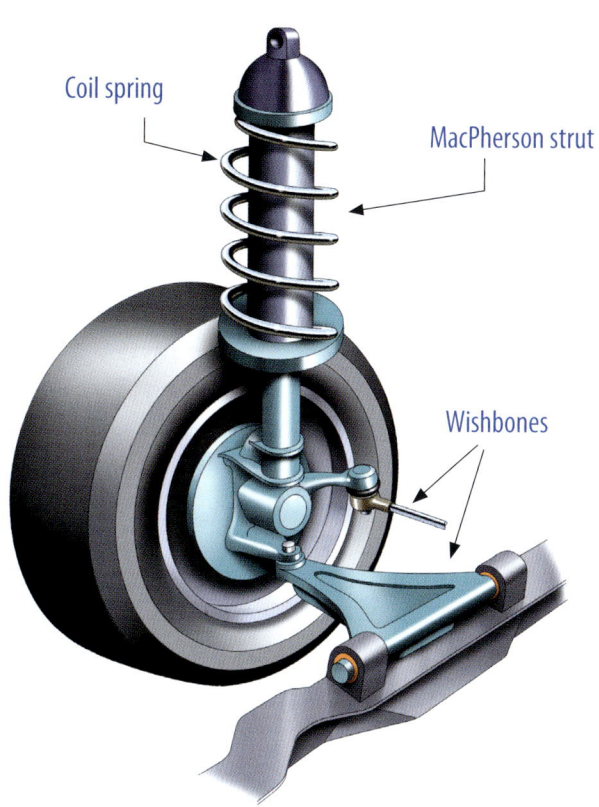

Even though the suspension system absorbs the shocks and jolts from the road, the wheels and tyres can still get damaged if they are driven over a stone or a pothole. When a vehicle has new tyres fitted they are balanced and aligned to allow the wheels to turn smoothly, and to ensure that the entire width of the tyre is in contact with the road surface. However, if a vehicle is driven fast on an uneven road or driven over a pothole, the alignment and balance of a tyre can be affected. This may cause a tyre to twist slightly, forcing one side of the tyre to have more contact with the road than the other, wearing its treads only on one side. This will affect the handling and balance of the vehicle during steering and braking as it may pull to one side.

It is important that tyres are regularly checked for signs of abnormal wear and damage. Foreign bodies, such as stones, glass, nails or thorns, can get stuck in the tyre. Tread depth should also be checked. Bald tyres with very little tread depth will lead to poor grip, especially in wet weather, as the tread's function is to disperse surface water to increase tyre grip and contact with the road. It is the driver's responsibility to ensure that the vehicle's tyres are in good condition. Failure to do so could lead to prosecution in the form of a fine and penalty points.

Tyre pressures should also be checked regularly to ensure that they function and handle as safely as possible while on the road. Tyres that are too hard can cause the vehicle to bounce off the road surface and may burst if they strike a sharp object, such as a stone. Tyres that are too soft can make steering more difficult. If you are unsure of your vehicle's correct tyre pressure you should check to see if it is written in your vehicle's operating manual, or on a panel somewhere inside your vehicle, or you can ask your mechanic for advice. You can then stop at a garage to check and inflate your own tyres with an air compressor.

The tightness of a vehicle's wheel nuts should be frequently checked using a proper shifting wrench to ensure that the wheels are safely and securely attached. Driving on uneven or poor road surfaces could make them come loose. To help reduce the amount of tyre wear motorists should:

- Keep to the recommended speed limits and drive with care.
- Keep tyres at the correct pressures.
- Avoid wheel spin when pulling off from a stationary position.
- Avoid heavy braking.
- Check tyres regularly for damage or foreign bodies.

FOR YOUR FOLDER

1. What is the gear arrangement in a car's steering called?
2. What is the function of the suspension system?
3. List three things that the suspension system can help provide.
4. What are coil springs and where are they used?
5. What are wishbones and in what part of the suspension system can they be found?
6. Where can leaf springs be found?
7. What is a MacPherson strut and where is it used?
8. What is the function of a shock absorber?
9. Explain how a shock absorber operates.

THE ENGINE LUBRICATION SYSTEM

The engine contains many metal surfaces rubbing against each other. Moving components within the engine can cause friction, heat and wear if oil is not used to ease their movement. A lack of oil can cause severe overheating causing parts to expand. If this is allowed to happen the engine could seize up, causing serious and expensive damage. Oil has three main functions:

- It reduces friction and overheating of moving parts.
- It reduces the level of wear as engine parts can move freely with ease.
- It helps to keep all the metal surfaces cool.

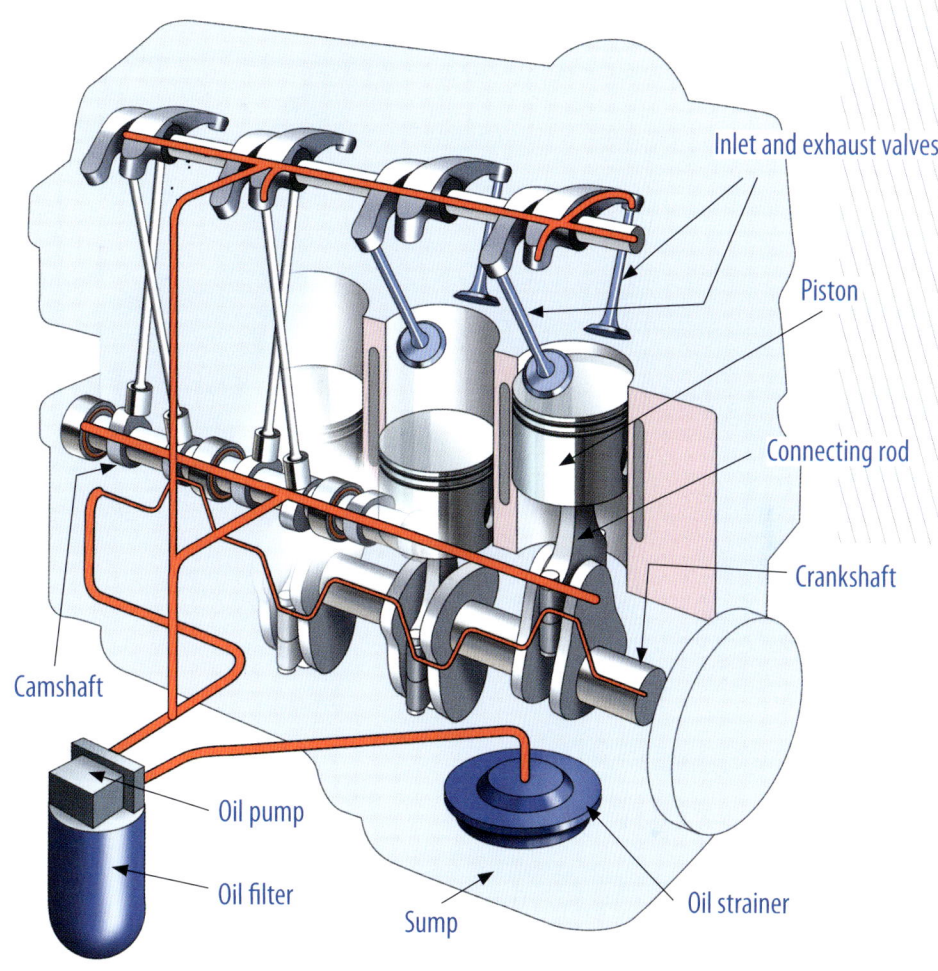

The level of oil in a vehicle should be checked weekly or before embarking on a long journey using the dipstick found under the bonnet. The dipstick and oil filler cap should be checked to ensure that they are on tightly and securely. Whenever the engine starts it can cause quite a lot of vibration, which could splash the oil around the engine. This which would make it dirty if the filler cap was off or the dipstick loose. As oil is essential for cooling and lubricating the engine's moving parts, the loss of oil could cause serious damage. Oil is stored in a sump at the bottom of the engine and is pumped around the various parts by an oil pump. When starting an engine from cold, particularly a diesel engine, you should wait for a moment to allow the oil to circulate before pulling off. The oil filter should be replaced regularly as it may become dirty with dirt or metal particles which could stop a good flow of oil. The oil should also be changed approximately every 5000 miles because it will gradually looe its thick and sticky characteristics due to the constantly high temperature in the engine.

Viscosity

A viscous liquid is one which is thick and sticky. Oil with low viscosity is a thin oil, while oil with high viscosity is a thick oil. The SAE (Society of Automotive Engineers) rate and grade oil by its level of viscosity. This is done by allowing a measured amount of oil to flow through a set diameter and timing how long it takes. The longer it takes, the higher the oil's viscosity will be. Oil with a high viscosity will be classified with a high number to identify it as a thick oil.

FOR YOUR FOLDER

1. What is the main function of the lubrication system?
2. What is the meaning of the term viscosity?
3. Where is oil stored?
4. Name two advantages of using oil in an engine.
5. What component is responsible for sending oil around the various parts of the engine?
6. Apart from lubrication, what is the other main function of oil?
7. Why is it not recommended to move off immediately after starting an engine from cold?

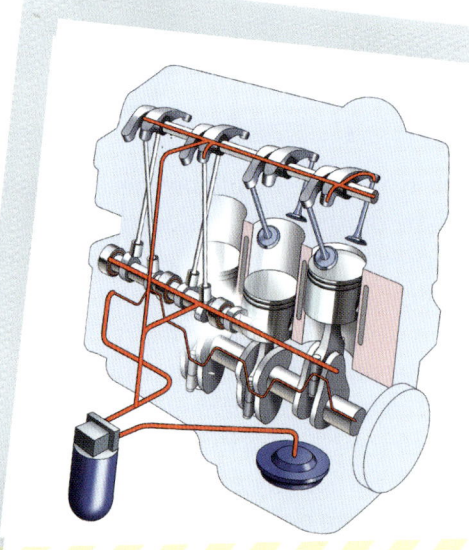

THE COOLING SYSTEM

There are two types of engine cooling systems:

- **Water cooling**
- **Air cooling**

The water cooling system is used in the engine. The engine is surrounded by numerous water passages for the following reasons:

- Water helps to reduce the noise from the engine.
- Water helps to keep the engine cool and maintains an even temperature.
- The hot water can be used in the car heaters.

The two main components for controlling the water temperature of an engine are the thermostat and the pressurised radiator cap. The pistons moving up and down inside the cylinders generate a lot of heat. These cylinders are surrounded by water jackets to help maintain an even temperature around each cylinder. A water pump is used to keep the water circulating around each part. The water pump can be either electrically driven by the battery or mechanically driven. The water pump is connected to the radiator fan, which draws air into the engine. They are connected by pulleys and driven by a fan belt, which is turned and rotated by the camshaft, located close to the crankshaft. If the temperature of the water gets too hot a thermostat will detect this. The function of the thermostat is to control the water temperature: when the water gets too hot, the thermostat will open to allow the water to flow through the top hose into a header expansion tank in the top part of the radiator. This header expansion tank is pressurised and allows the water to reach a boiling temperature of 110 degrees Celsius (°C). The radiator is made up of brass cooling fins to increase the cooling surface area. As the water passes from the top of the radiator to the bottom, a fan sucks the cool air in from outside, so that it passes over the top of the water hoses and cooling fins. This air cools the water, which flows out of the bottom of the radiator through the bottom hose and back into the water jackets around the cylinders.

Water cooling system

The main parts of the water cooling system are:

- **The radiator**
- **The water pump**
- **The thermostat**
- **The water jackets**
- **The heater**

These are shown on the next page.

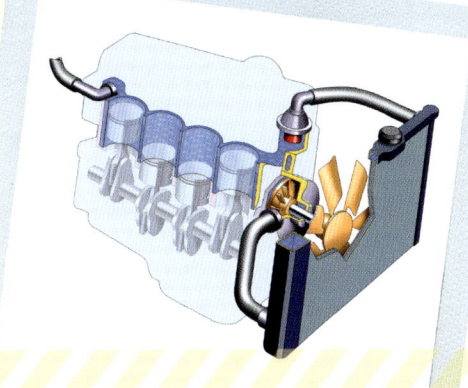

Water cooling system

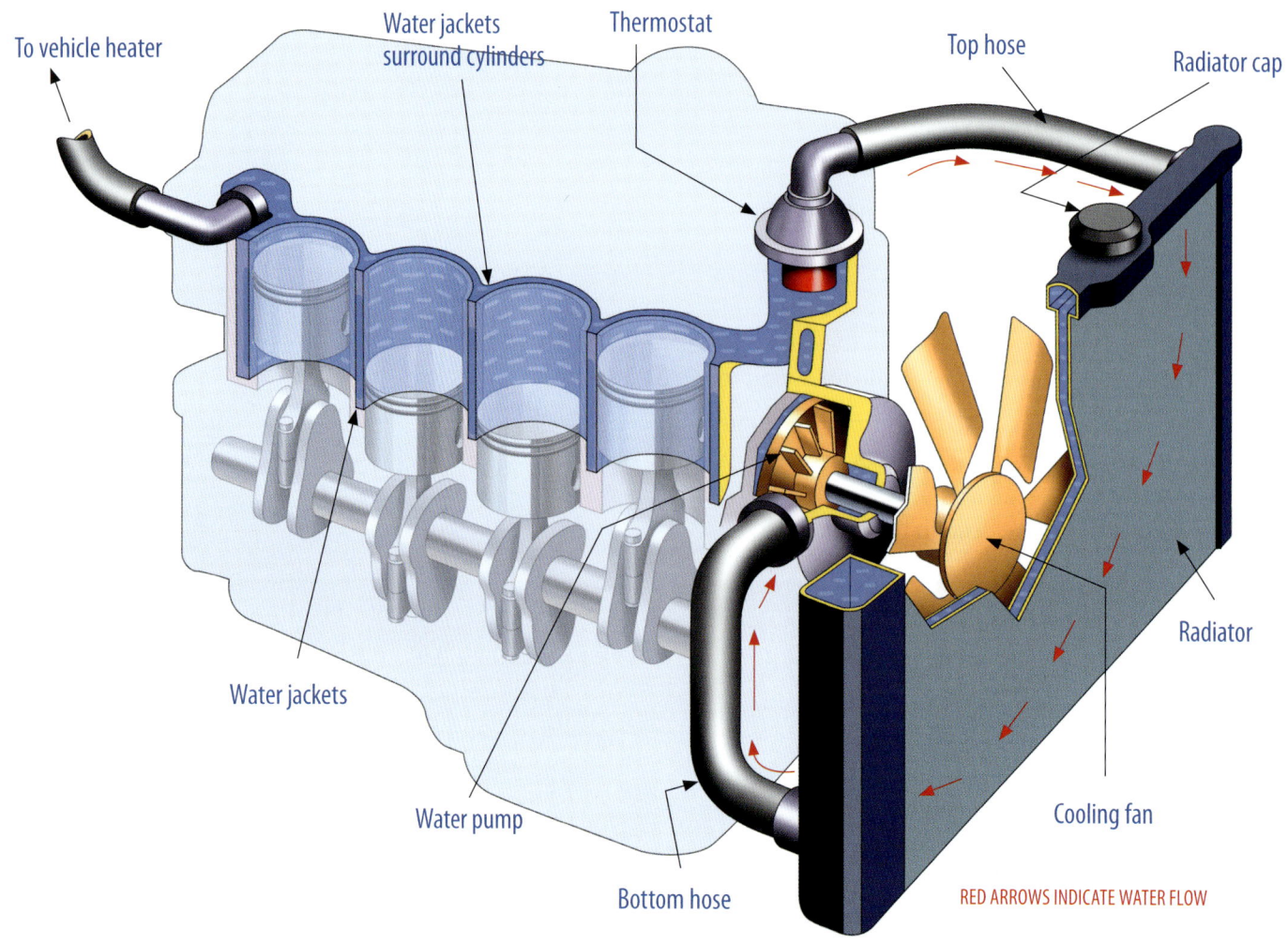

RED ARROWS INDICATE WATER FLOW

Some typical problems are associated with the water cooling system. The water can freeze, especially during the winter months, causing the radiator and hoses to burst or the cylinder block to crack. You should put anti-freeze into your engine's water system to prevent it freezing. The recommended level of anti-freeze is 30% anti-freeze to 70% water.

Leaks can also occur, resulting in reduced water levels and decreased pressure. A shortage of water (coolant) in the radiator will cause the engine to overheat because small amounts of water boil more quickly than large amounts. It is therefore important to frequently check the pipes and hoses, and the water level in the small float tank under the bonnet.

If the water pump fan belt (water pump drive belt) is loose the pump may not be circulating the water down through the radiator and the engine could overheat. You should regularly check the temperature gauge on your vehicle's dashboard to ensure that the engine's temperature is normal. If you hear your vehicle making a squealing noise it is likely that the fan belt is loose and needs tightened.

Engines run much better when they are warm (a temperature between 85°C and 110°C). Water usually boils at a temperature of 100°C, so the water in the engine is extremely hot. A pressurised radiator cap is positioned at the top of the radiator to seal it and pressurise the water. This means that the water will not boil until it is about 110°C. A spring valve is fitted underneath this cap. If the temperature rises too high, or the pressure becomes too great, the valve releases the built-up pressure by allowing water back into the expansion tank. If the temperature rises much more than 110°C the engine could overheat causing serious damage. The radiator could even burst. A sign of a vehicle overheating is steam blowing out from under the bonnet, i.e. coming from the engine.

Air cooling system

Air cooling systems are mainly used on motorcycles and mopeds. A water cooling system has cooling fins on the radiator but in an air cooling system the fins are directly connected to the cylinders to increase the cooling surfaces. A thermostat detects the engine overheating and reacts by opening a flap to allow in air from the atmosphere. A fan in the engine circulates the air over the fins and around the cylinders to reduce the temperature. Once the temperature is reduced the thermostat closes the flap to stop air flowing into the engine, allowing it to warm up again. This system works much better when the vehicle is moving as it improves the airflow. An air cooling system has a number of advantages: it is lighter than the water cooling system as it does not have to use or store water, and there is no water to leak or freeze. However, the air cooling system's main disadvantage is that it can be noisy. A water cooling system uses the water to help reduce engine noise. This is not possible in an air cooling system.

FOR YOUR FOLDER

7. What is the main purpose of the radiator cap?
8. Why is the cooling system pressurised?
9. Name the component in the cooling system which opens automatically when the engine gets too hot.
10. What damage can happen to an engine's cooling system if anti-freeze is not added to it during the winter months?
11. State two advantages of the air cooling system.
12. How does the air cooling system work?

FOR YOUR FOLDER

1. State three advantages of the water cooling system.
2. Why are the main parts of the engine surrounded by water in a water cooling system?
3. What is the function of the radiator?
4. How is the speed of water circulation increased?
5. Name the main parts of the water cooling system.
6. What is the purpose of the thermostat?

THE BRAKING SYSTEM

The braking system is one of the most important systems within a motor vehicle. It is used for slowing down and stopping. It is essential that all vehicles have good brakes to ensure the safety of the occupants and other road users. All vehicles have the following two braking systems:

- **The mechanical system (the handbrake)**
  - for parking
  - rear wheels only

- **The hydraulic system**
  - to slow down and stop a vehicle
  - front wheels – disc brakes
  - rear wheels – drum brakes } all four wheels

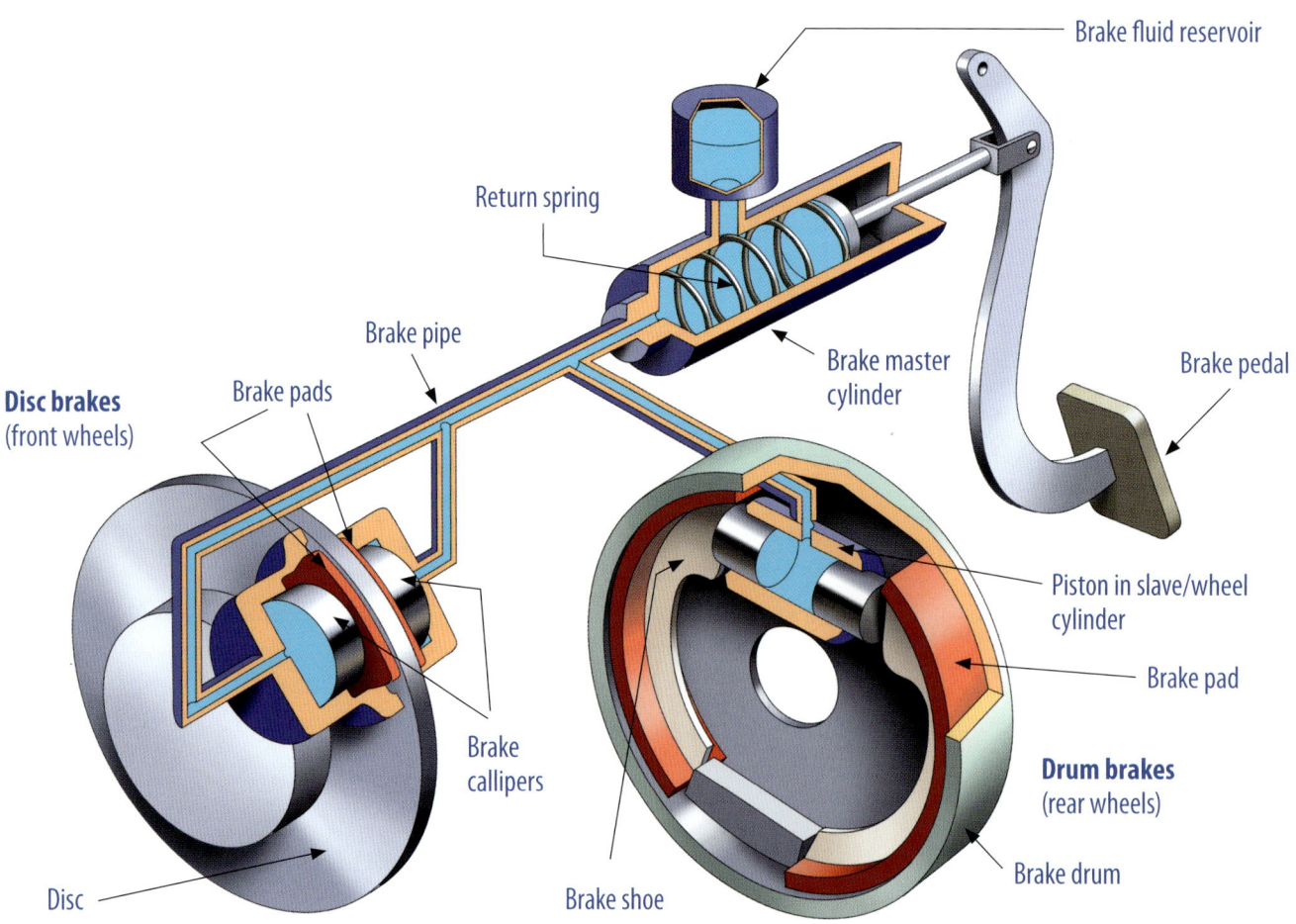

Main parts of the braking system

The hydraulic braking system uses brake pads which are connected to the wheel cylinder. These cylinders are filled with brake fluid, which forces the pads against the discs or drums, causing the wheels to slow down. The main components are as follows:

Brake pedal – This is a foot-operated lever inside the vehicle, which is used to slow down or stop the vehicle by operating on all of its four wheels.

Brake master cylinder – This main cylinder draws the brake fluid from a small tank, the brake fluid reservoir, found under the bonnet. It uses a piston to force the brake fluid through pipelines to each wheel when the brake pedal is pressed.

The brake servo – This unit determines how much brake pressure has been applied by the foot and allows the required amounts of brake fluid to flow to each wheel, slowing down or stopping the vehicle when needed.

Brake pipes – These pipes connect all four wheels from the brake pedal and master cylinder. The brake fluid flows through these pipes to all four wheels.

Brake shoes – In drum brakes, brake shoes are the part of the brake mechanism that moves towards the rotating wheels, slowing down or stopping the vehicle when the brake pedal is pressed. They move away from the wheel when the brake pedal is released.

Slave/wheel cylinders – In drum brakes, these cylinders are present in each wheel and contain pistons, which are connected to the brake shoes. The pistons are forced out by brake fluid to move the shoes against the rotating drums.

Brake drums – The rear wheels of the vehicle are connected to the brake drums. The drums rotate when the wheels rotate.

Brake callipers – These are strong metal casings that are only found on the disc brakes, on the front wheels. They are used to hold brake pads in place on either side of a rotating steel disc that is connected to the wheels.

Disc/brake pads – In drum brakes, the brake pads are positioned on top of the brake shoes. They are pressed and rub against the rotating drum, causing friction to slow down and eventually stop the vehicle. In disc brakes, the pads are located on either side of the steel disc and produce a pinching action when pressed against the disc, again causing friction to slow down and stop the vehicle.

Handbrake – This is a lever-operated brake found inside the vehicle. It is used for parking and is only applied on the back brakes.

It is important that the correct level of brake fluid is present to ensure that the brakes function properly. The level of brake fluid can be checked under the bonnet. A small dipstick is attached to the cap of the brake fluid reservoir to check the level of brake fluid. Brake pads generate friction and heat because they rub against a rotating disc or drum. These pads will eventually wear thin and will need to be replaced by a mechanic to restore the effectiveness of the braking. The hydraulic system's action is quiet, and only the brake pads need to be replaced.

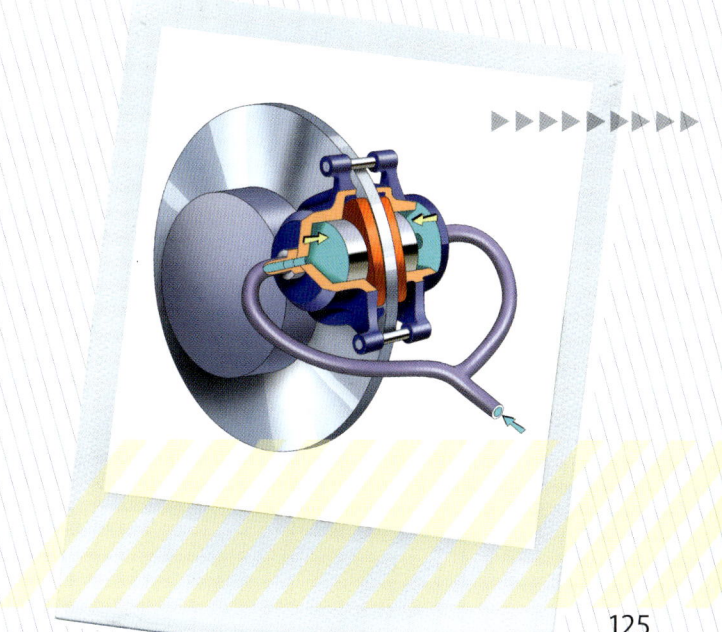

Disc brakes

These brakes are found on the front wheels, and sometimes on the rear wheels. The wheel is bolted to the brake disc. On pressing the brake pedal a piston in the master cylinder pushes the brake fluid along pipelines to force the brake pads, which are on either side, in against the rotating disc. The pressure applied causes a pinching action and will determine how quickly the discs stop rotating. Upon releasing the brake pedal a spring forces the piston back into the master cylinder. The brake fluid pressure is then reduced, releasing the force applied by the pads against the discs.

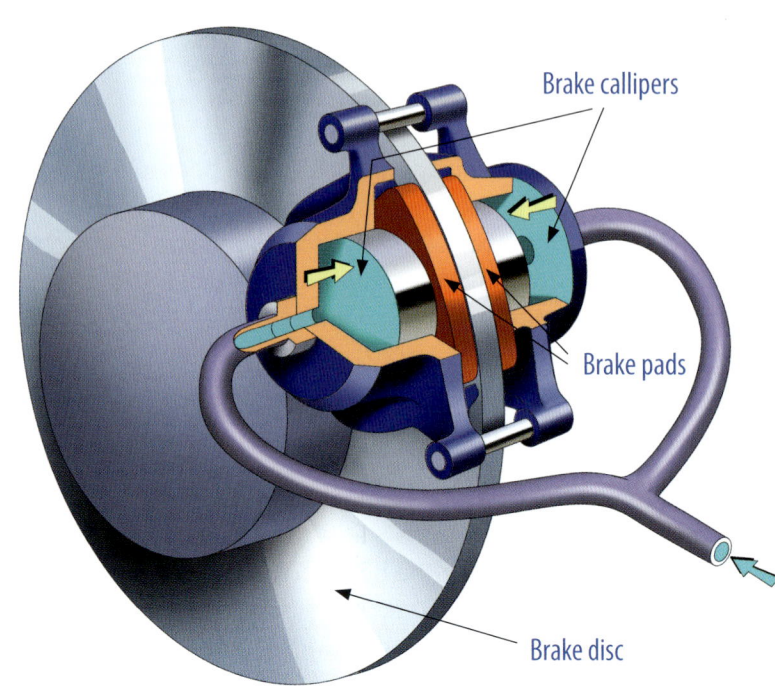

Drum brakes

Drum brakes are usually only found on rear wheels. The wheel is bolted to a drum that rotates. When the brake pedal is pressed, a piston in the master cylinder pushes brake fluid along pipelines to hydraulic cylinders contained inside the brake drum. These hydraulic cylinders have pistons connected to brake shoes that are lined with pads. The pistons force these shoes and pads out against the rotating drum, causing it to slow down and eventually stop. On releasing the brake pedal, springs pull the brake shoes and pads away from the drum, allowing the wheels to rotate again.

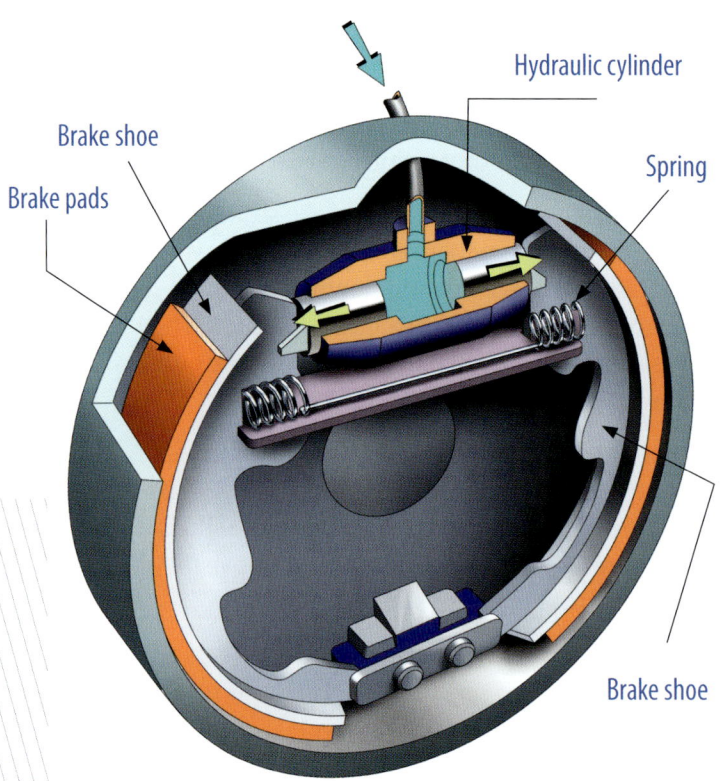

The mechanical system

The mechanical braking system is only operated by the handbrake. As its name suggests, the handbrake is applied by hand. It is located on the left hand side of the driver. It is only applied on the rear drum brakes and is used when parking or sitting stationary for a period of time, such as waiting at traffic lights.

Anti-lock braking system (ABS)

A 'locking' brake is one that has stopped the wheel from turning before the car itself has stopped moving, causing the tyre to skid. The letters ABS stand for anti-lock braking system, which is fitted to most modern cars. Each wheel has special sensors that detect a locking brake. It uses a pumping action to repeatedly apply, release and reapply pressure on the brakes. This repeated pinching action is carried out on each wheel to keep control of the vehicle and to prevent skidding. The vehicle should safely come to a halt.

FOR YOUR FOLDER

1. Why is the braking system considered to be a primary safety feature in a vehicle?
2. Briefly explain the function of the brakes.
3. Name two braking systems in a motor vehicle.
4. What does ABS stand for?
5. Name an advantage of the ABS braking system.
6. Briefly explain how ABS brakes work.
7. On what wheels does the hydraulic braking system operate?
8. Name two types of brakes used in the hydraulic braking system.
9. Briefly explain how drum brakes work.
10. Where on a vehicle would you find disc brakes?

USEFUL ABBREVIATIONS

A/C	Air Conditioning
ABC	Airways, Breathing, Circulation
ABS	Anti-lock Braking System
APR	Annual Percentage Rate
CO	Carbon Monoxide
DETR	Department of the Environment, Transport and the Regions
DOENI	Department of the Environment, Northern Ireland
DRDNI	Department for Regional Development, Northern Ireland
DVA	Driver and Vehicle Agency
E/M	Electric Mirrors
E/W	Electric Windows
FSH	Full Service History
HC	Hydrocarbons
HGV	Heavy Goods Vehicle
HP	Hire Purchase
LGV	Large Goods Vehicle
LPG	Liquid Petroleum Gas
LRP	Lead Replacement Fuel
MOT	Ministry of Transport Test
MSM	Mirror, Signal, Manoeuvre
NCPS	National Cycling Proficiency Scheme
ONO	Or Nearest Offer
PAS	Power Assisted Steering
PCV	Passenger Carrying Vehicle
PSNI	Police Service of Northern Ireland
PSV	Public Service Vehicle
RCL	Remote Central Locking
RRP	Recommended Retail Price
RTC	Road Traffic Collision
SAE	Society of Automotive Engineers
SORN	Statutory Off Road Notification
S/R	Sun Roof

INDEX

A

ABS (anti-lock braking system) 41, 127
Acceleration 76, 78, 108
Additional costs 74
Adverse weather 21, 30, 57, 89
Aerodynamic 56
Age 21, 27, 34, 35, 39, 47, 71
Agent 45
Aggression 34
Airbag 41, 55, 63
Air cooling system 123
Air filter 106, 107
Air quality 61, 69
Airway 86, 87
Alcohol 32, 33, 71
Alignment 53, 117
Alternator 93, 94
Ambulance 84, 87
Anti-freeze 122
Applicant 45, 72
APR 74, 75
Aquaplaning 25, 30
Assembly line 60, 61
Asthma 69
Authorised personnel 6, 10, 11
Autobahn 65
Autostrada 65

B

Baby carrier 55
Baffles 105
Balance (wheel) 53, 92, 117
Battery 60, 61, 93, 94, 95, 96
Black ice 29, 31
Bleeding 86, 87
Blind spot 19
Bloodstream 32, 33
Booster seat 55
Bounce test 117
Box junction 18
Brake fluid 92, 124, 125, 126
Brakes 124-126
Braking distance 25, 30, 40, 78
Breakdown 6, 20
Breathing 67, 68, 69, 85, 86, 87
Broker 44
Brow of hill 22

C

Camshaft 98, 99, 100, 119, 121
Carbon dioxide 68, 105
Carbon monoxide 51, 68, 69, 105
Carburettor 107, 108
Casualties 38, 85-87
Catalytic converter 69, 105, 106
Certificate 44, 45, 46, 48, 51, 73, 75, 76, 77
Charging system 93, 94
Child seat 55
Circulation 87
Claims 45, 46, 47, 82, 83
Clutch 76, 90, 98, 109, 110, 111, 112
Coil (electric) 95, 96
Cold weather equipment 25
Collapsible steering column 41, 63
Collision 10, 11, 21-23, 25, 28, 32, 35, 37, 38, 39, 41, 44, 55, 63, 66
Collision procedures 82-84
Colour blind 34
Combustion 100
Compensation 45, 67
Compression ignition 100, 104
Condensation 30
Congestion 7, 18, 23, 36, 57, 65, 66
Connecting rod 98, 99, 100, 102, 104, 119
Consciousness 85, 86
Contused wounds 87
Conviction 45, 46
Coolant 122
Cooling fins 121, 123
Cooling system 89, 94, 119, 121, 122, 123
Corrosion 57, 106
Costs (calculating) 45, 74-81
Cover note 45, 46
Crank 98
Crankcase 98
Crankpin 98, 99
Crankshaft 97, 98, 99, 100, 102, 104, 109, 110, 119, 121
Crosswinds 29, 31
Current (electric) 94, 95, 96, 97
Cut-out box 94
Cycle helmet 36, 56
Cycle track 13, 41
Cycling 6, 7, 11, 18, 24, 29, 31, 36, 42, 67, 71, 77, 78, 79
Cylinder 96, 98-105, 107, 108, 121, 122, 123
Cylinder block 98, 122
Cylinder head 98

INDEX

D
Damper 105, 106, 116
Dealers 74, 75, 77
Declined task 45
De-icer 29
Depreciation 60, 76, 77, 81
Depressant 32
Depression 34
DFI (Dept for Infrastructure) 43
Diesel 42, 60, 61, 62, 68, 92, 100, 104, 105, 119
Differential 109, 114
Dipped headlights 25, 27, 28, 30, 31
Disability 35
Disc brakes 25, 53, 124-126
Disengage 109, 110
Disqualification 32, 33, 42, 71, 72
Distractions 7, 29, 31, 34, 37-38
Distributor 95, 96
Documentation (legal) 48-52
Down payment 75
Drainage 41
Drinking and driving 21, 33, 42, 72
Driving licence 33, 46, 48, 49, 52, 75
Driving test 7, 34, 42, 43, 48, 49, 71, 72, 73, 75
Drowsy 26, 30
Drugs 33, 71
Drum brakes 124, 125, 126, 127
Dual-carriageway 10, 15, 41, 64
DVA (Driver and Vehicle Agency) 7, 48, 51
DVA Enforcement Officer 10, 11, 42

E
Education 42, 43
Electronic signs 10
Electrical system 93-97
Electric vehicles 50, 60, 61, 62
Electrolyte 94, 96
Emergency resuscitation 85
Emergency services 84, 85
Emissions 50, 51, 60, 62, 69, 105, 106
Endorsement 42, 48, 71, 72
Enforcement 42
Engaged 109, 110, 111, 112
Engineering 41
Engine management systems 92
Entitlements 48
Environmental effects 50, 60, 61, 66, 67-68
Excess (insurance) 45
Exemption certificate 55

Exhaust 51, 61, 68, 69, 92, 99, 100, 101, 102, 103, 104, 105-106, 119
Exhaust manifold 105
Expansion tank 121, 122

F
Fatigue 33
Final drive 109, 114
Finance companies 74, 75
Financial protection 44
Fire extinguisher 84, 88
First aid 83, 85, 87, 88
First party 44
Flood 26, 30, 106
Fluorescent 24, 25, 27, 36, 43, 83, 88
Flywheel 97, 98, 99, 109, 110
Fog 24, 27, 28, 30
Ford Model T 60
Foreign bodies 53, 86, 117, 118
Four-stroke engine 96, 99, 100, 101, 102, 104
Friction 53, 109, 111, 119, 125
Friction plate 59, 110
Frost 29, 31
Fuel 11, 42, 50, 60, 61, 68, 69, 76, 84, 95, 96, 98, 99, 100-104, 106-108
Fuel consumption 78
Fuel filter 76, 106, 107
Fuel injection 107
Fuel system 106-108
Full face helmet 56
Fully comprehensive 46
Funnelled wind 29

G
Gearbox 90, 98, 100, 109, 110, 111-112, 114
Gear ratios 113
Gears 35, 77, 78, 109, 110, 111, 112, 113
Glare 24, 26, 34
Gradients 41
Green card 46
Green Cross Code 42, 43
Grip 13, 25, 28, 30, 53, 78, 92, 117, 118
Gudgeon pin 98, 99, 101, 102, 104

H
Handbrake 51, 124, 125, 127
Harness 55
Hazard 11, 17, 20, 27, 34, 39, 83
Hazard warning plates 6, 14
Headlights 24, 25, 27, 28, 30, 31

INDEX

Head restraints 19, 41
Headwinds 29, 31
Heater 94, 97, 121, 122
Helmet 24, 36, 56, 77
Hidden dip 22
High-sided vehicle 29, 31
High tension leads 95, 96
Highway Code 6-7, 10, 12, 14, 16, 17, 18, 27, 40, 42, 55, 66, 71
Hire purchase 74
Hit and run 83
Horizontal deflection 39, 66
Hose 121, 122
Hydraulic braking system 60, 125-126
Hydrocarbons 51, 68, 69, 105

I
Ice 24, 29, 31
Ignite (fuel) 95, 96, 98, 99, 100, 101, 102, 104, 105, 107
Ignition system 84, 91, 93 95-97
Impacts 41, 46, 57, 58, 63, 87, 89
Incised wounds 87
Indemnity 45, 79
Indemnity fee 79, 80
Induction 100, 102, 104, 108
Injection *See:* Fuel injection
Injury 21, 37, 43, 46, 55, 83, 84, 85, 86, 87
Inlet manifold 106, 107, 108
Inlet valve 98, 99, 100, 102, 104, 107, 108
Insurance 33, 44-47, 48, 52, 72, 73, 75, 82, 83
Interest 74, 75, 76, 77, 79, 80
Internal combustion engine 59, 61, 89, 100

J
Jet style helmet 56
Junction 11, 18, 27, 38

K
Karl Benz 59, 61
Knock for knock 45

L
Lacerated wound 87
Law 27, 32, 42, 59, 69, 70-72, 79
Layshaft 111, 112, 113
Leasing 75
Legal requirements 6, 36, 44, 49, 51, 52, 53, 55, 75
Legislation *see:* Law
LGV (Large Goods Vehicle) 49

Licence *See:* Driving licence
Lighting up times 27
Lights 11, 24, 25, 26, 27, 28, 30, 31, 36, 41, 51, 53, 60, 63, 83, 96, 97
Linkage mechanism 110, 117
Loading restrictions 14
Loans 74, 75
LRP (Lead Replacement Petrol) 69
Lubrication 77, 98, 99, 111, 119

M
MacPherson strut 116, 117
Maintenance 41, 51, 57, 61, 78, 116
Manoeuvres 7, 18, 19, 24, 28, 31, 34, 35, 36, 37, 38, 42, 115
Manufacturers 56, 60, 63, 69, 73, 113
Mass production 60, 61, 63
Mechanical braking system 127
Mileage 74, 77
Mobility vehicle 35
Monthly repayments 74, 80
Moped 42, 48, 102, 114, 123
MOT 7, 26, 50, 51, 52, 72, 74, 76
MOT certificate 51, 73, 76, 77
Motorcycle 7, 11, 18, 19, 24, 29, 54, 56, 57, 71, 77, 114, 123
Motoring laws *See:* Law
Motoring costs 74-81
Motoring mathematics 73-81
Motorway 6, 8, 10, 13, 15, 20, 28, 29, 31, 33, 41, 61, 64, 65, 84
Mouth-to mouth 85

N
National speed limit 39
NCPS (National Cycling Proficiency Scheme) 36, 42, 43
Neutral 109, 111, 112
Newly qualified driver 49, 75
Nitrogen oxide 68, 69
No claims bonus 45, 47, 82
Noise pollution 62, 68, 70, 105
Non-endorsable 42, 71
Non-primary route 8, 65

O
Obstruction 19, 29, 83
Oil 76, 77, 92, 98, 99, 106, 111, 119, 120
Overheating 110, 119, 122, 123
Overtaking 6, 19, 29, 34, 39, 64

131

INDEX

P
Padded clothing 36, 77
Parking restrictions 42, 66
Pedestrians 7, 11, 18, 19, 22, 23, 24, 25, 26, 27, 29, 30, 31, 34, 35, 37, 38, 62, 66, 67, 68, 71
Pedestrianisation 66
Peripheral vision 34
Personal liability 45
Petrol engine 60, 69, 98-102, 107, 108
Petrol pump 98, 106, 108
Petrol tank 98, 106, 108
Policy 44, 45, 46, 48
Policy holder 44
Pollution 57, 62, 66, 67, 68, 69, 70, 105
Post-collision procedure 83-87
Power steering 115
Power stroke 96, 101
Practical driving test 7, 42, 75
Precautions 88
Premium 33, 44, 45, 46, 47, 48, 82
Pressure (tyre) 36, 53, 54, 78, 92, 118
Pressure plate 109, 110
Pressurised radiator cap *See:* Radiator cap
Primary routes 109, 110
Primary safety 8, 65
Primary shaft 41, 63
Primary signals 109, 110, 111, 112, 113
Proposal form 45
Proposer 44
Prosecution 21, 32, 33, 118
Protected bonus 45, 47
Provisional driving licence 48, 52, 71
Puncture (tyre) 53, 92
Puncture wounds 87
Purchasing cost 74-75, 79, 80, 81

R
Rack and pinion gear 115
Radiator 121-122
Radiator cap 121, 122
Rain 24, 25, 39, 30, 36, 64
Reciprocal/reciprocating motion 98, 100, 114
Recovery position 86, 87
Reflective clothing 24, 25, 27, 30, 36, 64
Reflective studs 15
Renewal notice 45, 46
Restricted driver 7, 42
Reversing 6, 19, 53, 65
Reverse gear 111, 113
Road markings 6, 12, 13, 16

Road narrowing 39
Road signals 6, 10, 11, 16, 18, 36
Road signs 6, 8, 9, 10, 14, 39, 64, 65
Road studs 13, 15
Road tax *See:* Vehicle Excise Duty
Road traffic collision 21, 22, 25, 37, 38, 41, 44, 63, 66, 82
Road works 6, 10, 19
Roundabouts 6, 11, 12, 13, 19
Running costs 57, 74, 76, 78
Rust 7, 77, 106

S
SAE (Society of Automotive Engineers) 120
SORN document 50
Safe grip 13
School patrol 14
School children 23
Seat belt 6, 21, 41, 42, 43, 51, 55, 63, 71, 72
Secondary safety 41, 43, 63
Secondary signals 11
Second-hand vehicle 73, 74, 77
Second party 44
Servicing 51, 76
Shock (medical) 83, 86
Shock absorbing 41, 90, 116, 117
Side impact bars 41, 63, 89
Signals 6, 10, 11, 16
Silencer box 105, 106
Single-carriageway 13, 65
Single track road 65
Slave/wheel cylinder 124, 125
Snow 24, 28, 31
Sound waves 105
Spark ignition four-stroke cycle 100
Spark ignition two-stroke cycle 102
Spark plug 95, 96, 98, 99, 100, 101, 102, 104, 107
Speed cushions 39, 66
Speed humps 39, 66
Speeding 21, 39, 42, 43, 66, 77, 78
Speed limits 6, 7, 10, 13, 39, 59, 64, 65, 66, 70, 78, 118
Splines 109, 110, 111, 112, 114
Standing costs 74
Starting system 93, 97
Stopping distances 6, 25, 28, 29, 31, 39, 40, 53, 78
Straight sale 73
Stress 32, 33, 34
Sulphur dioxide 68, 105
Sump 98, 119
Sun 26, 30, 34
Suspension 41, 51, 63, 78, 116-117

INDEX

T

Thermostat 121, 122, 123
Third party 44, 46
Top hose 121, 122
Traffic branch/division 39, 42
Traffic calming 39, 41, 66
Traffic collision *See:* Road traffic collision
Traffic congestion 18, 23, 33, 65, 66, 67
Traffic engineering 41
Traffic flow 10
Traffic lights 10, 11, 18, 34, 127
Traffic management 42, 64-66
Traffic signs *See:* Road signs
Transmission system 109-111
Transport (history of) 57-62
Travel graph 78-79
Tread 25, 53-54, 117
Tunnel vision 34
Two-stroke engine 100, 102-103
Tyres 25, 28, 30, 36, 41, 42, 51, 53-54, 63, 76, 77, 78, 92, 117, 118, 127
Tyre pressure 36, 53-54, 78, 92, 118

U

Underwriter 45
Universal joints 109, 111, 114
Utmost good faith 45

V

Valve 98, 99, 100, 101, 102, 104, 107, 108, 115, 119, 122
Vehicle engineering 41
Vehicle Excuse Duty (VED) 69
Venturi 108
Viscosity 120
Visibility 19, 24, 25, 26, 27, 28, 30, 31, 31, 35, 41, 53, 56
Vision 34
Vulnerable road users 21, 35, 36

W

Waiting restrictions 14
Warranty 73
Water cooling system 121-122, 123
Water jackets 121, 122
Water pump 121, 122
Wheel 13, 25, 29, 31, 53, 84, 114, 116-117, 118, 124, 125, 126, 127
Wheel arches 28, 31
Wheel/slave cylinder 125, 126
Wind 24, 29, 31, 36

GLOSSARY

ABS (anti-lock braking system) – part of the braking system that helps motorists to safely control and steer their vehicle while braking.

Aerodynamic – designed with rounded edges to reduce wind drag.

Agent – businesses looking to sell motor insurance.

Air filter – part of the fuel system that separates dust particles from the clean air, which is needed to mix with the fuel to power a vehicle.

Alternator – part of the electrical charging system to keep the battery charged and in a good live condition.

Aquaplaning – occurs when, in wet weather, the tyres of a vehicle rise up off the road onto the top of surface water, causing difficultly with steering and braking.

Assembly line – facilitates the mass production of the same vehicle in a short space of time.

Autobahn – German motorways with a speed limit of 81 mph.

Autostrada – Italian motorways with a speed limit of 80 mph.

Baffles – part of the exhaust system that restricts the flow of sound waves, reducing noise.

Battery – part of the electrical charging system that provides the main source of electricity needed to power all the lighting components, heaters, windscreen wipers and the radio in a vehicle.

Black ice – when rain falls and freezes on an already frost-covered surface. It is difficult to see and is often mistaken for a wet patch or puddle.

Blind spot – the part of the road that a driver cannot see from the driver's seat, even when using the mirrors.

Bounce test – a test carried out on a vehicle's suspension system.

Box junction – a traffic control system that allows drivers to enter an area only when their exit route is clear. These junctions are usually identified as large, yellow boxes with criss-cross lines, in which vehicles are not allowed to stop.

Braking distance – the distance a vehicle will travel from when the brakes are applied to where it comes to a complete stop.

Brake fluid – the liquid used in the braking system, which is used to transfer pressure from the brake pedal to each wheel when the brake pedal is pressed.

Broker/second party – the insurance company or insurance company's representative selling the insurance.

Brow of a hill – a dangerous part of the road where a driver's forward vision is restricted by a hill.

Carburettor – a part of the fuel system used in older cars that mixes the correct amounts of petrol and air together.

Camshaft – part of the engine, connected by a timing chain to the crankshaft. As it rotates it controls springs that open and close the inlet and exhaust valves.

Catalytic converter – a part of the exhaust system that helps cut down exhaust emissions.

Chicanes – a traffic calming measure used to reduce vehicle speeds.

Clutch – part of the transmission system that allows the gears to be connected or disconnected from the engine.

Contused wounds – bruising caused by being struck by a blunt instrument.

Cover note – a temporary insurance certificate covering the driver for 30–60 days while a permanent hardcopy of the certificate is being drawn up.

Crankshaft – part of the engine turned by the flywheel, causing the pistons to move up and down.

GLOSSARY

Crosswind – on open, exposed roads, such as motorways, bridges and carriageways, strong winds can cause vehicles, cyclists or pedestrians to sway.

Cut-out box – part of the charging system, this box acts as a switch, which sometimes needs to switch off automatically to prevent the battery from being over-charged.

Cylinder – tubes, very accurately formed to allow the four pistons to slide up and down precisely and freely.

Damper – part of the suspension system that slows down the movement of coil springs.

Declined task – when an insurance company refuses to pay a claim because of inaccurate personal information given by a client when applying for insurance cover.

Depreciation – the amount a vehicle de-values during ownership.

Depressant – a drug or liquid, such as alcohol, that slows the function of the central nervous system. By blocking some of the messages trying to reach the brain it alters perception, vision and hearing.

Differential – a part of the transmission system that allows one wheel to turn faster than the other when going round corners.

Distributor – part of the ignition system, this device passes a high voltage through high tension leads to the spark plugs.

Education – teaching the public and road users about road safety to help reduce and prevent accidents.

Electrolyte – a name given to the fluid found in battery cells, which helps to keep the battery in a good live condition.

Enforcement – authorised personnel applying the laws of the road to help reduce and prevent accidents.

Engineering – the construction and maintenance of roads, and the design and manufacture of vehicles that perform safely and provide as much protection as possible for their passengers.

Engine management system – built into most modern vehicles to detect any faults that may occur with the various operating systems. Mechanics can connect vehicles fitted with this system to a computerised machine in their garages to quickly detect the exact whereabouts and nature of the fault.

Fatigue – a term used to describe tiredness.

Final drive – part of the transmission system that allows the back wheels to turn.

First party/policy holder/proposer – see Policy holder.

Flywheel – a large, toothed wheel connected to the engine, which engages with the starter motor.

Foreign bodies – a term used to describe pieces of glass, stones or thorns that may get stuck in tyres.

Full service history – a record of all the maintenance checks carried out on a vehicle over the years by a mechanic.

Fully comprehensive – a type of insurance that covers all parties involved in an accident.

Funnelled wind – this is when wind is forced to travel through a confined area, concentrating the wind's power and increasing its strength. This can catch motorists, cyclists and pedestrians unawares, causing them to sway or topple over.

Gateways – a traffic calming measure used to slow down traffic on entering a residential built-up area.

Green Cross Code – safety information given to primary school children on the correct procedures for crossing a road.

GLOSSARY

Gudgeon pin – a pin that connects the piston to the connecting rod.

Hazard – anything that causes an obstruction or presents a danger to a road user.

Headwind – wind that slows down the movement of road users, especially affecting cyclists, motorcyclists and pedestrians.

Hidden dip – a dangerous part of the road where traffic may be concealed in a dip in the road while a motorist thinks they can see an entire, clear stretch of road ahead.

Hire purchase – a method of borrowing money from a finance company.

Horizontal deflection – a traffic calming measure used to slow down motorists.

Hydrocarbons – a pollutant found in exhaust emissions.

Incised wounds – these are open, cut wounds, usually made by a sharp object.

Indemnity – compensation from insurance companies restoring a person's financial position after an incident has occurred.

Inducements – special offers made to regular customers.

Induction – the drawing of fuel or air into a cylinder.

Inlet manifold – the part of the fuel system which distributes fuel to the individual cylinders.

Internal combustion engine – any engine that operates by burning fuel inside the engine.

International Motor Insurance Card – motorists need to produce this document to enable them to drive in countries outside the EU.

Lacerated wounds – these are caused by impact, resulting in a crushing of bones, and a ripping and tearing of flesh.

Leaf springs – these are steel strips mounted on top of each other, which are found in rear wheel suspension systems on older cars.

Leasing – renting a vehicle, through monthly payments.

Lighting up times – times when street and vehicle lights are supposed to be switched on.

MacPherson strut – the most commonly used front wheel suspension system.

Mass production – large quantities of the same product manufactured.

Mechanical braking system – the operation of the handbrake.

NCPS – a programme set up in primary schools to educate children in cycling safety.

No claims bonus – a percentage reduction in the cost of insurance for having made no claims.

Pedestrianised zone – an area that is free from vehicles allowing pedestrians to move around freely.

Peripheral vision – a person's side vision, an ability to see things outside their direct line of sight.

Personal liability – accepting responsibility for causing a road accident and what you are personally responsible for paying.

Policy holder/proposer/first party – any motorist with, or looking for, insurance.

Power steering – a system that allows the wheels to be turned without any real force.

Premium – the price you have to pay for insurance cover.

Primary safety – relates to the features that help a vehicle perform safely under everyday driving conditions.

GLOSSARY

Proposer/first party/policy holder/ – *see* Policy holder.

Punctured wound – wounds caused by something sharp piercing the skin.

Recovery position – to place someone onto his or her side, with the chin forward and the hand underneath the cheek, and to tilt the mouth downwards, allowing any fluids to drain out of the mouth and to prevent a casualty from swallowing the tongue. . The position is used if a casualty is unconscious.

Renewal notice – a notice sent out by the insurance company to state that your insurance is about to expire. It will include a new start date and the cost for the next term.

Road studs – these help motorists to identify their road position in the dark. There are four different colours of studs: amber, red, green and white.

Running costs – the day-to-day costs of owning a motor vehicle.

SORN document – a legal document to state that a vehicle is being kept off the road, without paying Vehicle Excise Duty.

Safe grip – a coloured surface material on the road which provides additional grip to vehicles, helping them slow down more safely. It is also used on cycle tracks or at the entrance to residential areas to indicate a 30 mph speed limit.

Secondary safety – relates to features that help to protect a vehicle's occupants when it is involved in a collision.

Second party/broker – *see* Broker.

Side impact bars – a feature of secondary safety, these bars are inserted into the door panels of a vehicle to improve passenger protection.

Silencer box – located in the exhaust system, it reduces noise pollution by slowing down the airflow, lowering gas pressures and therefore noise.

Spark plugs – these provide a spark to ignite the fuel in the engine.

Speed cushions – a traffic calming measure used to encourage reduced vehicle speeds.

Stimulant – a drug or liquid that makes you feel happy and more confident, affecting your awareness and reaction times.

Straight sale – the buying of a vehicle without trading another in against it.

Sump – where oil is stored at the bottom of the engine.

Thermostat – part of the water cooling system used to control the temperature of the water around the engine.

Third party – any person or road user other than the driver who has been involved in an accident.

Third party insurance – this type of insurance covers the driver if they damage the property of, or injure, a third party while driving. It does not cover any damage caused to the driver or vehicle they are driving.

Third party fire and theft – this type of insurance is exactly the same as third party, with the additional benefit that it also allows the driver to claim if the car is stolen or set on fire.

Tunnel vision – the loss of peripheral vision, where the focus is circular and restricted.

Underwriter – an insurance company employee who makes a risk assessment and decides whether or not to accept an insurance proposal.

Universal joints – part of the transmission system that allows flexibility of the drive or propeller shaft, allowing for circular and up and down movements.

Utmost good faith – describes a person who has acted honestly with regards to an insurance claim.

GLOSSARY

Vehicle Excise Duty (VED) – a tax that must be paid on every vehicle using public roads. Sometimes incorrectly called 'road tax'.

Viscosity – a term used to describe the quality and characteristics of different types of oil.

Vulnerable road users – the young, the elderly, the disabled and non-motorised road users who are all more vulnerable on the road than vehicle drivers who are fit and able. This is because of their inexperience, physical restrictions or lack of a safety framework protecting them.

Warranties – a guarantee, which often comes with new vehicles, covering the cost of repair for vehicle faults and malfunctions during a specified period of time.

Water jackets – water passages that surround the cylinders in an engine to help maintain an even temperature.

Water pump – the part of the water cooling system that keeps the water circulating around the engine.